VANISHING POINTS

Martin Jones

BROADWAY PLAY PUBLISHING INC

357 W 20th St., NY NY 10011
212 627-1055

© Copyright 1985, 1993 by Martin Jones

All rights reserved. This work is fully protected under the copyright laws of the United States of America. No part of this publication may be photocopied, reproduced, stored in a retrieval system, or transmitted, in any form or by any means, electronic, mechanical, recording, or otherwise, without the prior permission of the publisher. Additional copies of this play are available from the publisher.

Written permission is required for live performance of any sort. This includes readings, cuttings, scenes, and excerpts. For amateur and stock performances, please contact Broadway Play Publishing Inc. For all other rights contact Scott Hudson, at Writers & Artists Agency, 19 W. 44th St., Suite 1000, New York, N.Y. 10036, 212 391-1112.

The Snowman: from COLLECTED POEMS by Wallace Stevens. Copyright 1923 and renewed 1951 by Wallace Stevens. Reprinted by permission of Alfred A Knopf Inc., 201 E 50th St., NY NY 10022. Permission for any use of *The Snowman* must be obtained from Alfred A Knopf Inc.

First printing: March 1993
ISBN: 0-88145-096-0
Book design: Marie Donovan
Word processing: Microsoft Word for Windows
Typographic controls: Xerox Ventura Publisher 2.0 PE
Typeface: Palatino
Printed on recycled acid-free paper and bound in the USA.

ABOUT THE AUTHOR

Martin Jones is the Resident Playwright/Dramaturg with the Mad Horse Theatre Company of Portland, Maine, where four of his plays have premiered: VANISHING POINTS (1987), YOU CAN'T GET THERE FROM HERE (musical revue, 1988), SQUATS (1989), and DARK RIVER (1992).

Martin Jones' published plays include SNOW LEOPARDS (Samuel French), WEST MEMPHIS MOJO (Broadway Play Publishing), and OLD SOLDIERS (*Best Short Plays of 1983*).

In 1986, he received a Rockefeller Foundation Grant in Playwriting, and worked that year as Resident Playwright for the Portland Stage Company, where his children's play, THE KANGAROO'S TALE, was staged and then toured throughout the state.

His play WEST MEMPHIS MOJO was a winner in the 1986 FDG/CBS New Plays Award Program. The play premiered at the Northlight Theatre in Evanston, Illinois, in March 1986. It has been produced frequently by professional theatres throughout the United States and Canada, including a successful run at New York's esteemed Negro Ensemble Company in 1988. It is currently under development for a feature film by Propaganda Films.

In 1991, Jones co-authored the screenplay for the HBO/Lorimar film PRISON STORIES: WOMEN ON THE INSIDE, which had its premiere at the 1991

Sundance Film Festival, and was originally broadcast on HBO in January 1991. The film was nominated for an Ace Award in the "Best Dramatic Special" category.

Another of his feature film scripts, SECOND SKIN, has been optioned recently, and he is currently working on both plays and screenplays.

ACKNOWLEDGMENT

The writing of this play would have been impossible without the cooperation of the artist, Elizabeth Peak. I would like to thank Ms. Peak for having the courage to face, and share publicly, the painful memories of her family tragedy that formed the background for VANISHING POINTS: On September 9, 1972, retired Army Colonel William Oliver Peak, his wife, Bernice, and their fourteen-year-old daughter, Barbara, were found murdered in their home in Grand Island, Nebraska. Twenty years later, at this writing, their murders remain an unsolved mystery. The play is dedicated to their memory.

ORIGINAL PRODUCTIONS

VANISHING POINTS had its world premiere at the Mad Horse Theatre Company in Portland, Maine, on 23 April 1987, with the following cast and creative contributors:

BETH	Lisa Stathoplos
BARBARA/VICKI	Terry Drew
WALTER/CLIFF	Walt Dunlap
CAROLYN/PEG	Cynthia Barnett
LENNY/CAZ	Randy Aromando
FRAN	Deborah Hall
GARY	John Philbrick
POLICEMAN/SINFELD	Donald Jellerson
Direction and production design	Michael Rafkin
Stage manager	Ginger Myhaver
Managing director	Karl Rogers
Sound design	Cliff Rugg
Photography/poster design	Stephen Fazio

VANISHING POINTS had its West Coast premiere at the International City Theatre in Long Beach, California on 14 October 1988, with the following cast and creative contributors:

BETH .... Judith Borne
BARBARA/VICKI .... Hilary Green
WALTER/CLIFF .... Tom Simcox
CAROLYN/PEG .... Bobbi Holtzman
LENNY/CAZ .... Matth Wisterman
FRAN .... Arlette Stella Poland
GARY .... David Nieman
POLICEMAN/SINFELD .... Ty Smith

Producer .... Shashin Desai
Director .... Peter Grego
Set designer .... Don Gruber
Lighting designer .... Paulie Jenkins
Costume designer .... Cathy Crane-McCoy
Make-up designer .... Barbara Matthews
Original music .... Chuck Estes
Production stage manager .... Diana Jensen

CAST OF CHARACTERS*

The play should be performed by no more than eight actors, four men and four women. Certain roles are doubled for the purpose of thematic echo. The characters of BETH, FRAN, and GARY are not doubled.

BETH—Early 20s. An artist.
FRAN—Early 30s. Her sister. Married to GARY.
WALTER—57, their father. Runs a tree nursery.
CAROLYN—51, his wife.
BARBARA—14, BETH's sister.
CLIFF—55, WALTER's brother. A police buff.
GARY—36, FRAN's husband. A businessman.
LENNY—Mid-20s. BETH's boyfriend.
VICKI—18, a street vendor in California.
PEG—50, she runs an artists' colony in the Mojave Desert.
CAZ—Late 20s. A rattlesnake hunter in the desert.
SINFELD—35, a detective.
POLICEMAN—34, local cop in Kearns, Nebraska.

*Suggested role doubling: WALTER/CLIFF, CAROLYN/PEG, BARBARA/VICKI, LENNY/CAZ, SINFELD/POLICEMAN.

Setting: An open stage with platform levels. There should be no major scenery, only simple tables, chairs, and props as called for in the script. The action of the play occurs in many locations conjured up in the memory of BETH. Time: The mid-1970s.

I was the world in which I walked, and what I saw
Or heard or felt came not but from myself;
And there I found myself more truly and more strange.
—Wallace Stevens

Midway in our life's journey, I went astray
from the straight road and woke to find myself
alone in a dark wood. How shall I say
what wood that was! I never saw so drear,
so rank, so arduous a wilderness!
Its very memory gives a shape to fear.
—Dante, *Inferno I*, John Ciardi, translator

ACT ONE

(An open space with platforms to define areas of the stage. On the floor, near center, the white chalk outlines of three human bodies, similar to those used in homicide investigations.)

(At rise: BETH *stands near the center. She looks at the chalk outlines on the floor.)*

BETH: I keep having this dream about my parents' house. I've come home to draw a picture of the house, yet, for some reason, I don't want to go inside. *(Pause)* But, somehow, in the dream—I'm already inside the house. Nothing moves but currents of air as I pass through familiar rooms. Now the light is changing. Edges are growing fuzzy—dissolving—all dots and random lines. Something catches my eye in the corner of an empty bedroom. A stain on the floor—like paint was thrown. *(*BETH *kneels by one of the chalk outlines.)* I can't make out the shape. A face? A flowering plant? The shadow of a tree? But, there is no tree. It's one... now two...now three shapes...all overlapping. *(*BETH *touches one of the chalk outlines and begins to feel tired, as if it draws the energy from her body.)* The light is fading. And I'm so sleepy all of a sudden. I can barely hold my head up. It feels as heavy as a bucket of water. But, if I sleep now I'll never finish the drawing in time...and there isn't any time left. *(*BETH *lies down in one of the chalk outlines. Piano music filters in.)* Barbara's in the parlor...practicing scales. It's so far away, and I can hear my parents' voices...whispering. They're at the table...ready for church...I hear an old car coming up the road. *(Sound of a car approaching, very softly)* A rattling noisy muffler...and I try to call them. I open my mouth, but no sound comes out. They're far away, in another part of the house...they couldn't hear me even if I screamed. And the car engine grows louder, then stops...a car door slams...and it's too late. I can't do anything to warn them. I can't move my arms, I'm so tired...and I can't wake up again...ever....

(BETH curls her body into a sleeping position inside one of the outlines. A hymn played on the piano drifts in. Lights change. BARBARA enters what represents the front porch of the house. She scuffs her heels on the porch step, then stops, and looks down the road that leads to the house.)

BARBARA: Dad! Dad! Somebody's coming up the road to the house.

WALTER: *(Off)* Who is it?

BARBARA: I don't know.

WALTER: *(Off)* What kind of car is it?

BARBARA: Some ol' junky blue car.

(WALTER enters, dressed for church.)

WALTER: Who is it?

BARBARA: I dunno...but they're coming here.

(CAROLYN enters the porch area, also dressed for church.)

CAROLYN: Is that Uncle Cliff's car?

WALTER: No.

CAROLYN: Well, who is that?

WALTER: I don't know.

BARBARA: They're getting out.

CAROLYN: What do they want?

WALTER: I don't know.

CAROLYN: Who are they?

ACT ONE

(The family stands motionless, staring out at the road. Image freezes. Piano music fades in. Lights fade. Lights up on BETH, *moaning in her sleep.)*

BARBARA: *(Off)* Beth, get up. C'mon.

CAROLYN: *(Off)* Beth, wake up. We're going to be late for church.

LENNY: *(Off)* Beth, wake up.

*(*BETH *moans again. Lights up in another area—a table set for breakfast.* WALTER, CAROLYN, BARBARA, *and* LENNY *are seated at the table.)*

BARBARA: I'm hungry. Can we start now?

CAROLYN: As soon as your sister comes to the table.

WALTER: Where is she? Is she awake?

BARBARA: No.

LENNY: Want me to rouse her, Mr. Perkins?

WALTER: *(Rises from table.)* No, Lenny. I'll do it.

CAROLYN: I've never seen anyone sleep so much.

LENNY: Every weekend...at school...we used to sleep late. *(He realizes his faux pas.)* I mean Beth would...at her dorm, I mean.

*(*CAROLYN *pours a coffee in silence.)*

BARBARA: Pass the muffins, please.

*(*WALTER *has crossed to* BETH's *area. He stands, watching her sleep. He claps his hands loudly.* BETH *wakes suddenly.)*

WALTER: Time enough, Missy. You're not on vacation anymore.

BETH: It's Sunday.

WALTER: That's right. Time for church. If you get moving, we'll just make the late service.

BETH: Why do I have to go to church? I never went once when I was away at college.

WALTER: Do it for your mother, so we have peace in this house. Okay?

BETH: It's hypocritical for me to go.

WALTER: Uh-huh! We'll say a prayer this morning for forgiveness. Now, get dressed. There's coffee and muffins if you hurry. Lenny's waiting downstairs.

(WALTER *leaves, returns to the table area.* BETH *sighs, rubs her face.*)

WALTER: *(Sits at table)* She's coming.

BARBARA: I was hoping she died in her sleep.

WALTER: Barbara!

BARBARA: *(Contrite)* Yes, Sir.

(WALTER *gives her a look. She stops buttering a muffin, sets it down. The family clasps hands around the table. They bow their heads to pray.* LENNY *hesitates, then follows suit.*)

WALTER: Heavenly Father, watch over us, and bless the food which we are about to receive....

(BETH *joins them at the table.* CAROLYN *is annoyed that she has interrupted the prayer.*)

CAROLYN: Just sit down, please.

(BETH *sits.*)

WALTER: ...with all thy goodness and mercy. Amen.

BARBARA: Amen! Pass the orange juice, please.

CAROLYN: *(To* BETH*)* You're late. We've missed the 9:30 service.

BETH: Sorry. I overslept.

CAROLYN: Lenny was up early. Why can't you get up?

BETH: I dunno. I was very tired. Pass the coffee, please.

WALTER: You were out kinda late last night.

BETH: It was only twelve-thirty.

ACT ONE 5

CAROLYN: One-thirty.

BETH: Was it?

WALTER: Where were you two?

BETH: Dad, I'm over twenty-one.

CAROLYN: You don't have to get defensive.

WALTER: I'm just asking a simple question.

LENNY: We were at the lake, Mr. Perkins.

WALTER: Thank you, Lenny.

CAROLYN: At that hour? What were you doing?

(BARBARA snickers, mimes smoking a joint. BETH glares at her.)

BETH: Barbara, would you like some hot coffee in your face?

WALTER: Bethany!

BETH: Yes, Sir...sorry.

(They eat in silence. CAROLYN changes the subject.)

CAROLYN: Yesterday I ran into Ed Walker at the mall. He asked about you, Beth. Said he's still waiting for your answer.

BETH: I know. I forgot to call him.

CAROLYN: *(After a pause)* Well, you know he's not going to hold that job for you all summer.

BETH: I know.

CAROLYN: Did you know that your old friend from junior high...Millie Whitaker...Carla's sister...you remember the Whitaker girls, don't you?

(BETH nods, eats hunched over.)

CAROLYN: Beth, would you please sit up when you eat. You look like a coal miner shoveling it in when you sit all hunched like that. *(BARBARA snickers.)* Anyway, Millie started off as a secretary over at

"Green Giant" soon as she finished college...did quite well...worked her way up, and now she's the head purchasing agent for the entire county.

BETH: Good for Millie. She belongs in the *(Singing to* LENNY*)* "Valley of the ho, ho, ho...Green Giant"!

*(*LENNY *and* BARBARA *laugh.* CAROLYN *is not amused.)*

CAROLYN: I gather you're not interested in working.

BETH: I was just making a joke.

CAROLYN: So what are we supposed to tell Ed Walker if he calls?

BETH: I'll call him, okay? Maybe tomorrow.

CAROLYN: You're not going to take the job, are you? *(*BETH *sighs heavily.)* Why must you turn up your nose at every good opportunity?

BETH: Maybe I don't wanna be a secretary at "Green Giant"....

WALTER: Carolyn, will you leave her alone. We're at the table.

CAROLYN: Walter, I'm just inquiring about what she's planning to do with her life. I don't think that's such an unreasonable thing to ask. Is it, Beth?

BETH: *(After a long pause)* I was thinkin'...maybe I want to paint...professionally.

BARBARA: Oh, not this again.

BETH: Barbara, shut up!

CAROLYN: Well, I think that's wonderful. Beth, have you found this painting job yet? Is someone going to pay you a living wage for this?

BETH: Not yet. I said I was just thinking about it.

CAROLYN: I see.

(Silence around the table. WALTER *tries to lighten the mood.)*

ACT ONE 7

WALTER: Well, I could call Bud Petersen. He's got a crew out painting houses this summer. I'd give you a brush and roller to get started. *(Everyone laughs except* BETH.*)* You said you wanted to paint.

BETH: That's not funny.

WALTER: Oh, Beth, I'm just kidding you.

*(*BARBARA *laughs harder.)*

BETH: Barbara, cram it!

CAROLYN: Bethany, I think you're over-reacting.

BETH: You never take me seriously. I'm just a big joke. Ha, ha, ha!

CAROLYN: That's enough.

*(*BETH *sulks, picking at her plate of food. Uncomfortable silence.* LENNY *rises.)*

LENNY: If you'll excuse me...I'm, uh...gonna go work on my bike. Nice breakfast, Mrs. Perkins.

*(*LENNY *exits.* BARBARA *starts to clear dishes from the table.)*

CAROLYN: Just put those in the sink for later. We have to get dressed, or we'll be late. Are you ready, Beth? You're not going like that.

BETH: That's right. I'm not going.

*(*BARBARA *makes a face at* BETH, *and exits with the dishes.* CAROLYN *stares at* BETH.*)*

BETH: My soul will not burn for eternity just because I don't feel like going one lousy Sunday.

CAROLYN: Just change your clothes.

BETH: Lenny and I are staying here. I promised Dad I'd repot some seedlings in the nursery.

CAROLYN: Walter, can't she do that some other time? *(*BETH *rises and starts out.)* Where are you going?

BETH: Down to the greenhouse. Goodbye! Have fun at church.

CAROLYN: Bethany!

BETH: *(Off)* Oh, lay off!

(CAROLYN looks at WALTER.)

CAROLYN: This happens every Sunday.

WALTER: Ease up, Carolyn. You've been on her back all morning.

CAROLYN: The only reason she's acting this way is because of Lenny. Showing off...that's what she's doing...ever since he came back here....

WALTER: Not so loud. He might hear you.

CAROLYN: The only reason she won't go is so they can be alone while we're at church. You know what will happen the minute we leave this house, and don't tell me you don't.

WALTER: All right...I'll talk to her.

CAROLYN: I'm fed up with this behavior.

WALTER: Go on, get dressed. I'll take care of it.

(CAROLYN exits. WALTER lights a cigarette with a Zippo lighter. Lights change. BETH is in the greenhouse, replanting a small shrub. LENNY sits nearby. They are sharing a joint. WALTER approaches the doorway. LENNY hides the joint, and moves lazily out the door. WALTER stands there, smells the air.)

WALTER: You burning some peat moss down here? *(Pause)* Your mother is pretty upset.

BETH: So am I, but that doesn't seem to count for anything.

WALTER: I guess I made a lousy joke at the table. I was just trying to lighten the mood.

BETH: Why is she picking on me so much this summer?

ACT ONE

WALTER: Oh, she doesn't mean everything she says. Your mother's going through some difficult changes...with Fran living in Chicago, you away at school for four years...and, well, it won't be too long before Barbara grows up...I guess she feels kinda... alone....

BETH: I hope I die before I go through menopause.

WALTER: Just try to be patient, okay?

BETH: How many of these shrubs need repotting?

WALTER: Three dozens for the courthouse...and we'll need to make up four wreaths for the funeral home.

BETH: Okay.

WALTER: Don't forget to add new soil on those pines...and fresh water.

BETH: I know...I know.

CAROLYN: *(Off)* Walter, where are you?

WALTER: I'm in the greenhouse.

CAROLYN: *(Off)* Don't you be working in that dirt. You've got your Sunday suit on. Walter, do you hear me?

WALTER: Yes, I hear you.

CAROLYN: *(Off)* Is Beth out there with you?

WALTER: Yes.

CAROLYN: *(Off)* Is she dressed yet? I don't want to be late.

BETH: I'm not going. That's final.

WALTER: It's going to be a long summer if you don't bend a little.

CAROLYN: *(Off)* Walter, are you coming? We're leaving in ten minutes.

*(*WALTER *looks at* LENNY, *who is lingering in the doorway.)*

WALTER: Lenny, do me a favor. Go tell her I'll be there in a couple of minutes.

CAROLYN: *(Off)* Walter, are you getting your clothes dirty?

WALTER: And tell her I'm not covered in potting soil, okay?

LENNY: Sure, Mr. Perkins.

(LENNY lingers at the door for a moment. He looks at BETH.)

LENNY: I wanna go for a ride in a while, okay?

BETH: Sure.

(LENNY exits.)

WALTER: Not very talkative is he?

BETH: I doubt he can get a word in around this house. *(Pause)* You don't like Lenny very much, do you?

WALTER: I never said that.

BETH: You know, he's actually very sensitive, and he does pick up on the vibes.

WALTER: Lenny's always welcome in this house. I've never said anything to the contrary.

BETH: As long as the subject of cohabitation never comes up again, right? I wish I'd never told her. Me and my big mouth. Lord save us from any unpleasantness that might upset her delicate sensibilities.

WALTER: I don't think that's very fair, Beth.

BETH: Nothing I do is quite good enough for her.

WALTER: Beth!

BETH: Well, it's true. She can't wait to get me out of the house, shuffled off to the "Green Giant" secretarial pool...living in some crappy one-bedroom duplex over by the mall....

ACT ONE

WALTER: You don't have to work there. You can stay here and help out at the nursery. It'll be the same thing you've been doing every summer since junior high. And I'll pay you as good wages as you'll find anywhere around....

BETH: You're missing the point, Dad. I said I'd help out here, but you can't expect me to grow trees for the rest of my life.

(WALTER *is a bit taken aback.*)

BETH: *(Pause)* Lenny asked me to come back to New York with him. *(Pause)* You know there's nothing for me here.

WALTER: And what are you going to do for money?

BETH: Money? Is that all you guys ever think about?

WALTER: You gotta eat, Beth. You gotta pay rent somewhere.

(BARBARA *enters, exasperated.*)

BARBARA: Mom sent me down to get you. Will you guys come on before she throws a total conniption.

WALTER: In a minute.

BETH: Where's Lenny?

BARBARA: He's sitting on his stupid motorcycle like he's James Dean or something. He's so weird.

BETH: He wants to leave. Tell him to wait for me.

BARBARA: I'm not telling him anything.

WALTER: Barbara, your mother's calling you.

BARBARA: No, she's not.

WALTER: Go on back to the house.

BARBARA: I wanna stay here.

WALTER: Barbara!

BARBARA: Okay, okay, I'm going. What shall I tell Mom?

WALTER: I'll be there in a minute.

BARBARA: Oh, brother! *(She exits.)*

WALTER: Beth, sometimes I feel like we never get to see you. You're always gone somewhere with Lenny. Is it that hard for you to spend any time with your family? *(BETH shrugs. Pause.)* At one time, I thought we had an understanding about the business. A nursery is a family sort of thing. It's not like a 7-11 store, you don't just get some stranger to come in and take it over. I thought you liked this work.

BETH: I do like it, but....

WALTER: I'm not going to be around forever. I'd like to know that things are run the way they're supposed to. We talked about this, Beth.

BETH: Dad, that was back in high school. I was just a kid. Back then, I agreed to it, bacause it made you happy. *(Pause)* I'm sorry...maybe you should have asked Fran to take it over.

WALTER: Fran has her own life.

BETH: Oh? And I don't? I see how it is.

(Sound of LENNY's *motorcycle revving off stage.* CAROLYN *calls out.)*

WALTER: This is going to kill your mother.

CAROLYN: *(Off)* Walter, I'm leaving in two minutes.

BETH: Don't drag her into it. Why can't you just admit that you are the one it hurts? Well, I hurt too!

WALTER: You're so selfish.

BETH: Oh, stop it! Just stop it! All of you!!! *(*BETH *storms out.)* Lenny, wait for me. Let's get out of here.

WALTER: Where are you going?

BETH: I need some air!

WALTER: Beth! Wait a minute! Come back here! Beth!

ACT ONE

CAROLYN: *(Off)* Walter!!!

(BETH is gone. Sound of motorcycle pulling away quickly. WALTER watches them go. Engine sound dies away. BARBARA enters.)

BARBARA: Why'd Beth run off? Do we still have to go to church now?

WALTER: Yes.

BARBARA: Why?

WALTER: Because your mother wants us to.

BARBARA: And what do you want?

(WALTER does not answer. He goes into the house. BARBARA stands for a moment on the porch. She begins scuffing her heels on the porch steps. She stops, and looks down the road from the house.)

BARBARA: Dad...Dad... Somebody's coming up the road to the house.

WALTER: *(Off)* Who is it?

BARBARA: I don't know.

WALTER: *(Off)* What kind of car?

BARBARA: Some ol' junky blue car.

WALTER: *(Re-enters porch.)* Who is it?

BARBARA: I dunno...but, they're coming here.

(CAROLYN enters the porch, dressed for church.)

CAROLYN: That's not Uncle Cliff's car!

WALTER: No.

CAROLYN: Well...who is that?

WALTER: I don't know.

CAROLYN: What do they want?

(The family stands motionless, staring at the road. Sound of an approaching car as the lights fade on them.)

(An open field under a starry sky. LENNY *and* BETH *are huddled together on a blanket on the ground. They have been getting high. They look up at the stars.)*

LENNY: Man, I'm ripped! Wow! Look at those stars!

BETH: *(Lying back)* Really beautiful. *(Points)* Look... there's the Big Dipper...and Cassiopeia...over there.

LENNY: Who?

BETH: Cassiopeia. The Lady on the Throne.

LENNY: Oh, right.

BETH: See that bluish one? Now, if you follow that line of stars down over there, you'll find the Scorpion.

*(*LENNY *puts his hand under the blanket and grabs her playfully.)*

LENNY: And you'll find the crab under here!

BETH: *(Laughing)* Lenny! Stop! Don't tickle me...please...don't. Look at the stars.

LENNY: *(Lying back)* Boy, I sure like it out here at night...only thing I miss since I moved to New York...the open sky and a full moon.

BETH: That's the only thing?

LENNY: Okay...sometimes I miss you too.

BETH: *(Slugs his arm)* Sometimes?

LENNY: Ouch, that hurt! Hey, I was only joking! *(He kisses her lightly.)* This is the same place we made love the first time. Remember?

BETH: *(Sarcastic)* No, I forgot.

LENNY: Right over by those sycamore trees...in your old man's car. The Buick.

BETH: It was a Mercury.

LENNY: You sure? I thought it was the ol' blue bomber.

BETH: Nope. The 1967 Mercury. Must have been someone else in the Buick, huh?

ACT ONE 15

LENNY: Maybe so.

BETH: Who?

LENNY: Nobody. Hey, eleventh grade...we were both virgins. Well, at least I was. *(BETH playfully pushes him down. They roll around, tickling each other.)* Okay...okay...you win...stop tickling me...I can't stand it...I'll pee my pants...you gotta stop! *(BETH stops. He gets up and stretches.)* What a night! *(He takes out a lid of grass from his knapsack on the ground.)* I got one more joint rolled. Wanna do it?

BETH: Not me. I'm wasted.

LENNY: *(Lights the joint)* Party pooper. Guess I'll do a few hits.

BETH: What time is it?

LENNY: I dunno...after eleven, I think.

BETH: We should be heading back.

LENNY: A few more tokes.

BETH: My folks are gonna be pissed.

LENNY: They were pissed when we left. Nothing new, huh? *(Acting like Cheech and Chong)* Wow! This is some righteous stuff...like, hey man, this dope is so fine...why, you can barely....*(He pretends to nod out.* BETH *giggles.* LENNY *joins in.)*

BETH: You idiot! We should be going.

LENNY: Where did you get this weed?...It's incredible!

BETH: Home grown..."Nebraska Red."

LENNY/BETH: *(An old joke)* GO BIG RED!! *(*LENNY *collapses, laughing.* BETH *starts to fold the blanket. He grabs the blanket.)*

LENNY: Let's make love again.

BETH: Not now...c'mon, help me fold this blanket.

LENNY: Why don't we slip off to the lake...go skinny dippin'.

BETH: It's too cold.

LENNY: I want some time alone...just the two of us....

BETH: We've been alone all day.

LENNY: I wanna stay out all night and party.

BETH: We can't.

LENNY: *(Mimicking)* "We can't. It's almost midnight. I have to go home." *(BETH shoots him a dirty look.)* You know, in New York people don't even go out to dinner until after ten.

BETH: The rest of the world doesn't give a damn what you do in New York.

LENNY: Hey, I thought you wanted to live in New York.

BETH: *(Sighs)* I don't know.

LENNY: Oh? This is news to me. I thought you couldn't wait to get the hell out of Soybeanville. Hey, what have we talked about all summer? Huh? Why did I come out here to see you? It's what we planned.

BETH: I know.

LENNY: So? You broke the news to your old man. The worst is over. I don't see what the big problem is.

BETH: Everybody seems to know what I should do, everybody except me.

LENNY: With a degree in studio art, nobody's exactly standing in line out here to give you a job...unless of course maybe you wanna do illustrations of tractors for the John Deere catalogue.

BETH: Lenny, don't push! Okay?

LENNY: Okay, take your time. Think it over. Just don't take all year to make up your mind. That's all I'm sayin'. *(BETH folds the blanket, silently. LENNY watches*

ACT ONE 17

her.) Okay...I didn't mean for that to sound like an ultimatum. Well, say something. Anything. *(Pause)* Okay, you're pissed off. Let's hear it. *(BETH freezes; she sees something in the distance.)* What's wrong? What are you looking at?

BETH: I just saw someone over there, below those trees. Look there.

LENNY: Holy shit! There's a light. Somebody's coming up here.

BETH: Look, now there are two lights coming this way. Is it a car?

LENNY: No. There's no road over there. It's flashlights. Hey, it's cops. They're coming right toward us.

BETH: Oh, God, where's the grass?

LENNY: In my knapsack!

BETH: Quick, toss it!

LENNY: Too late...they've seen us. Don't run...don't panic...just stay calm.

(They stand still. Two bright flashlights approach. CLIFF *and a* POLICEMAN *appear.)*

POLICEMAN: We're looking for a Beth Perkins. Is she up here?

BETH: Yes, that's me.

CLIFF: Yep, that's her, Officer. Oh, God, Beth. I'm so glad you're okay.... Oh, Jesus...you're okay.

*(*CLIFF *throws his arms around her.)*

BETH: Of course I'm all right. What's wrong? Uncle Cliff, what are you doing up here?

POLICEMAN: Miss Perkins, there's been an accident.

BETH: Accident?

CLIFF: Oh, honey. It ain't no accident. It's your Mama, and Walter, and Barbara. Somebody killed them. They've been shot.

(BETH *stares at them for a moment, then she laughs, thinking they are kidding her.*)

BETH: You're joking.

(CLIFF *and the* POLICEMAN *shake their heads "No."* BETH *starts to back away from them.*)

CLIFF: No, honey. I wish I was....

BETH: No. Tell me you're...pullin' a trick. You're making it up. Tell me.

POLICEMAN: *(After a pause)* No, Ma'm. Sorry. It's the truth.

(BETH *looks from one to the other. Their faces are set and grim.* BETH *feels panic.*)

BETH: Oh, no...God...no...please.

CLIFF: Carolyn's still alive...just barely.... Oh, God, I'm so sorry.

BETH: *(Backing away)* No...no... Nooo! *(Screams)* NO!

(BETH *collapses on the ground. The men stand over her.* CAROLYN *appears in a spotlight in another part of the stage.*)

CLIFF: C'mon, honey...get up, please.

CAROLYN: Bethany Perkins, you get down out of that treehouse. Right this minute. You hear me?

BETH: No, Mama, no...

CAROLYN: Get down here, and wash your hands. Supper is waiting, young lady.

BETH: Mama.

CAROLYN: Do you want your father to get his belt after you? Now get in the house.

CLIFF: Beth, you have to get up. We have to go.

ACT ONE 19

BETH: No...I can't....

CLIFF: Boys, you better help me get her up on her feet.

(The men help her to her feet, as the light fades.)

(Upstage, in a separate spotlight, CLIFF appears, seated in a chair. He begins his testimony as if he is relating the story to the police. CLIFF focuses directly to the audience.)

CLIFF: When they didn't show up, I stopped by the house after church. Ealier that morning I had talked to Carolyn on the phone. They were plannin' to stop by after the service, and we'd all watch a ball game on my new color TV...like we did every Sunday. *(Pause)* When I pulled in their drive...I sensed somethin' was odd, 'cause Merridoc...that's their dog, see...an ol' Labrador...
well, Merridoc wasn't tied up in the side yard, and the door was standin' wide open. I went on in the house...
same as usual, but the TV was on...loud...and all the lights were on in the middle of the day. I thought that was strange, 'cause I know how frugal Walter was about wastin' electricity. And then, there was that damned ol' dog, Merridoc. He was pacin' up and down the hall leadin' to the bedroom. He was whimperin' like somethin' was wrong in the bedroom. I turned off the TV and called for Carolyn...then Walter, but no answer, so I went through the family room on into the living room...and then I saw the blood. It was shaped like the dog's footprints...leadin' down the hallway. I followed the trail of prints to their bedroom. I saw a crumpled heap of arms and torso lying next to the bed. Took a minute to realize that it was a person I was lookin' at. It was Carolyn. The ol' dog was lickin' a wound on the side of her face...and there was a big dark stain spreadin' out on the floor from under her head.
I crossed to the other side of the bed...where they got

this French door...kinda thing...you can look out past the cottonwoods...on down to the greenhouse, and it was there by the door I found Walter. He was lyin' on his side...an unlit cigarette still in his mouth...his right arm outstretched toward the door...his old Zippo lighter still in his hand. Looked like he was about to light a cigarette, and then somebody shot him in the back of the head...up close. I ran in to the kitchen to phone the Sheriff...that's where I found Barbara...by the kitchen door...like she was tryin' to get away, 'fore they caught her...shot twice in the back...poor girl...she was so young.... I called the Sheriff, and then went back in the bedroom. Carolyn's purse was on the bed...money and credit cards still in it...I was lookin' around, and that's when I heard Carolyn moan...just a little...and
I knew she was still alive...my God, I scooped her up and carried her out to my car...and I tore up the mailbox goin' out of the drive. I rushed her over to the emergency room.... Christ, you never saw so much blood. *(Pause)* I don't understand it. They were good people...and they never hurt nobody. It makes you think...it could happen anywhere...any time.... *(Pause)* I know one thing...folks are gonna be keepin' their doors locked from now on, yessir. It's a terrible thing.

(Lights fade on CLIFF. BETH *and* LENNY *are in separate spotlights. The* POLICEMAN *conducts his interrogation from an area between their two chairs.)*

POLICEMAN: What were you doing out in that field?

BETH: Watching the stars. Hey, look, I've been here for hours. I want to see my mother. Please, let me go, okay?

POLICEMAN: Where have you been for the past twelve hours?

LENNY: I don't know.

ACT ONE

POLICEMAN: You don't know?

LENNY: I can't remember everything I did all day.

POLICEMAN: Where do you live?

LENNY: New York...now. I used to live in Kearns.

POLICEMAN: When?

LENNY: Grade school...high school. I grew up here...then my parents moved.

POLICEMAN: Did your father have any enemies?

BETH: None that I know of.

POLICEMAN: Where were you?

BETH: Lenny and I went for a ride on his motorcycle.

POLICEMAN: All day?

BETH: Yeah...and then we just sorta hung out, okay?

POLICEMAN: Are you the owner of the motorcycle?

LENNY: Yes.

POLICEMAN: Do your parents ever lock the doors of the house?

BETH: No...never.

POLICEMAN: Do you ever use drugs?

BETH: Uh...I...in college...I used to get high...sometimes.

POLICEMAN: Have you ever sold drugs?

LENNY: Never.

POLICEMAN: Have you got a valid driver's license?

LENNY: Yeah, I got a New York license.

POLICEMAN: And you were away from the house for how long?

BETH: All day...since morning.

POLICEMAN: And you never came back?

BETH: No. My father and I had an argument...so, I left.

POLICEMAN: You have a previous arrest record for narcotics possession.

LENNY: Is that so?

POLICEMAN: In 1972 and 1974. Possession for less than one ounce.

LENNY: Both of those cases were dismissed. I was acquitted. Look it up.

POLICEMAN: Do you use drugs now?

LENNY: Not me. I learned my lesson the last time I got busted.

POLICEMAN: We found a small quantity of marijuana in your knapsack.

LENNY: I have no idea how it got there.

POLICEMAN: What did you argue about?

BETH: Family stuff. Nothing important.

POLICEMAN: What are you doing in Kearns?

LENNY: I told you. I came to see my girlfriend.

POLICEMAN: Can you elaborate?

BETH: My father doesn't like Lenny...and we argued.... Okay?

POLICEMAN: Did you have an argument with Mr. Perkins?

LENNY: No.

POLICEMAN: Did you get along with Mr. Perkins?

LENNY: Sure. Great pals.

POLICEMAN: Did Lenny make any threats against your father?

BETH: No! Look, he didn't do it...we were together all day. Are you listening to me?

POLICEMAN: You drove your motorcycle over a thousand miles to see an old girlfriend?

ACT ONE

LENNY: Yes, I did. Something wrong with that?

POLICEMAN: Where does your sister live?

BETH: A suburb of Chicago. Evanston, Illinois.

POLICEMAN: The registration of this motorcycle expired in April.

LENNY: Oh, no. Are you kidding me?

POLICEMAN: Does your father keep a safe or large amounts of cash at the house?

BETH: I don't know if he kept money at the house. I don't live there all the time. I've been away at school. I'm visiting over the summer.

POLICEMAN: Does your father keep a gun in the house?

BETH: I don't know. *(Pause)* I think he used to have a pistol, but I haven't seen it for years.

POLICEMAN: You didn't get along well with Mr. Perkins, did you?

LENNY: What are you getting at? Hey, I never hurt anyone, okay? You are really wasting a lot of time if you think I had anything to do with this.

BETH: Look, I want to get the hell out of here! I want to see my mother. She's in the hospital. When will you stop asking me all these questions? I wanna get out of here! Please...

POLICEMAN: All right. You're free to go.

(Lights fade on the chairs. Lights up in another area—the waiting room of a hospital. FRAN, BETH's *older sister, sits with a wadded Kleenex in her hand. She has been crying.* GARY, *her husband, enters, sits next to* FRAN.*)*

FRAN: Did you find out anything?

GARY: They said they had just released her. They're bringing them over now.

FRAN: Why did they hold her so long? Damn them! Did you tell her?

GARY: She'd already left when I called.

FRAN: Oh, God. How am I gonna tell her?

GARY: Just tell the truth.

(BETH *and* LENNY *enter, accompanied by the* POLICEMAN. FRAN *and* BETH *embrace.*)

FRAN: There she is. Oh, Beth...

BETH: Frannie. Oh, it's good to see you. And Gary...

(BETH *and* GARY *embrace.*)

GARY: We've been here for hours. Waiting for you.

BETH: They just let us go. Where is she? Is she okay? (FRAN *looks at* GARY. BETH *notices the awkward glance.*) What's the matter? Uncle Cliff said she was gonna be okay. What's wrong?

FRAN: Beth...uh...

GARY: There were complications...she was in surgery for three hours. A lot of hemorrhaging in the brain...the excess pressure on the brain was....

BETH: I want to see her. Just for a few minutes. I don't care if she's sleeping. I just want to be with her....

FRAN: We lost her, Beth. I'm sorry.

(BETH *stares at them, anger rising.*)

BETH: When? When did she die? When?

GARY: About two hours ago...you were still being interrogated.

FRAN: We tried to call you, but...they said that....

(BETH *turns with rage at the* POLICEMAN.*)

BETH: Did you hear that? YOU SON OF A BITCH! She was dying in here...YOU FUCKER!!!

(BETH *flails wildly at the* POLICEMAN. GARY *and* LENNY *try to calm her.*)

GARY: Beth! Don't...please...Beth.

LENNY: Beth, easy...Beth. Don't...you'll hurt yourself. Beth!

BETH: You bastard!

(BETH *collapses on the floor.* FRAN *kneels by her, and holds* BETH *in her arms, rocking her gently.* LENNY *and the* POLICEMAN *look on helplessly.*)

FRAN: Somebody call a doctor! Beth...Beth. Poor Bethany. I'm so sorry, baby.

POLICEMAN: I'm terribly sorry...we didn't know....

GARY: Haven't you done enough? Why don't you just get the hell out of here!

POLICEMAN: Sorry, Sir.

(He leaves. GARY *kneels next to* FRAN *and* BETH. GARY *looks at* LENNY.*)*

GARY: Would you go see if you can find a nurse, or a doctor?

*(*LENNY *nods and exits.* FRAN *holds* BETH *gently, as her crying subsides.* BETH *looks off to one direction.)*

BETH: Mama...don't go....

*(*CAROLYN, WALTER, *and* BARBARA *appear in light in another part of the stage.* FRAN *and* GARY *fade into shadows.* BETH *sits alone in a spotlight on the floor. She looks at her family.)*

CAROLYN: Too late, Beth. We're leaving without you.

BETH: No...

WALTER: It's time to go to church. Is your sister awake?

BARBARA: I can't get her up. She won't wake up.

WALTER: All right, then. It's too late.

BARBARA: She didn't even try.

CAROLYN: You know what I would have really liked, Beth? A portrait of the family. All of us together, to hang over the sofa.

WALTER: Forget it, Carolyn. You're wasting your time. She isn't even listening.

BETH: I'll do it. Just give me a chance. Don't go.

WALTER: Too late.

CAROLYN: Too late, Beth.

BARBARA: All gone.

BETH: No. Don't leave me. Not yet. No...

(Lights fade on CAROLYN, WALTER, and BARBARA. Light changes in BETH's area. Sound of knocking on a door. BETH sits up. FRAN enters.)

FRAN: Beth, are you all right?

BETH: Yes, I'm okay.

FRAN: I heard you calling out.

BETH: I must have been talking in my sleep.

FRAN: Yes. Feel any better?

BETH: My head hurts...and my arms. I feel real groggy.

FRAN: They gave you a sedative at the hospital. You've been sleeping on and off for the past two days.

BETH: What time is it?

FRAN: Around five in the afternoon. Today's the funeral service. Do you feel up to it?

BETH: I think I'll be all right. Boy, does my arm hurt. I must have made quite a scene.

FRAN: I would have done the same thing. Don't worry about it.

BETH: I'm dizzy.

FRAN: Are you sure you're all right?

BETH: Yeah, I'm okay. Hungry.

ACT ONE

FRAN: There will be food afterwards. Everyone's downstairs, ready to go. They're waiting on us.

BETH: Just give me a minute. I gotta do something with my hair.

(BETH *looks at herself in the mirror, starts to brush her hair. In another part of the stage,* CAROLYN *and* BARBARA *appear in light.* CAROLYN *is brushing* BARBARA*'s hair. Soft piano music floats in.*)

BARBARA: Will you teach me to play the piano?

CAROLYN: I tried to teach your sister, but Beth didn't have the patience.

BARBARA: I have the patience. I'll study hard, and practice all the time.

CAROLYN: We'll see.

BARBARA: I love it when you brush my hair. A hundred strokes everyday.

CAROLYN: You have fine, beautiful hair, Barbara.

BETH: *(Lowers her own brush)* Mama...brush my hair, too.

CAROLYN: I can't, Beth.

BETH: My hair, please...

(CAROLYN *continues to brush* BARBARA*'s hair.*)

CAROLYN: Beth, there's nothing I can do with your hair. The brush gets all tangled in snarls. It's hopeless.

(FRAN *stands behind* BETH, *takes the hair brush, and begins to brush* BETH*'s hair.*)

BETH: Mama...

CAROLYN: Barbara has such beautiful hair. Long, silky...soft to touch.

(*Lights fade on* CAROLYN *and* BARBARA. FRAN *finishes with* BETH*'s hair.*)

FRAN: That's the best I can do. Is that okay?

BETH: *(Sad)* Yes. Thanks.

FRAN: Why is your hair so different? Dad used to say you must have been the milkman's daughter, huh?

BETH: Yes.

FRAN: Well, are you ready? *(BETH nods.)* We have to go now. They're waiting.

(Lights change for the funeral. A row of metal folding chairs face the audience. BETH and FRAN move slowly down to the chairs and sit, facing front. A hymn is played on a church organ throughout the scene. FRAN and BETH speak their thoughts at the funeral, directly to the audience.)

FRAN: A small, low-ceilinged, multipurpose building. Fluorescent lights. A cement floor. Three flower-covered coffins lined up facing rows of metal folding chairs. A podium with a wreath.

BETH: It could be anywhere...a showroom of new cars...a bowling alley...a P.T.A. meeting...anywhere, except for those three shiny, oblong boxes.

FRAN: The faces in the folding chairs, all turning toward you as you file past to the front row.

BETH: The stares...the whispers..."That's them...there's the daughters."

FRAN: A church elder was chosen to speak the eulogy.

BETH: An abstract sermonette on the randomness of death.

FRAN: Is there any dignified way to say goodbye?

BETH: The crowd of stunned neighbors...quietly saying to themselves, "Thank God, it didn't happen to me...thank God."

FRAN: Family friends...distant relatives I haven't seen since childhood....

BETH: Lenny in a borrowed black suit. His trousers were too short. He couldn't button the top button on

ACT ONE

the shirt. One of Uncle Cliff's old ties, hanging loose around his neck. Lenny never owned a tie.

FRAN: Cousin Becky, and her husband, from Laredo...

BETH: Strong-willed Baptists...

FRAN: Aunt Flo...heavily powdered, smelling of lilacs in her new purple hat...

BETH: She looked like an African violet under the harsh lights.

FRAN: The funeral director asked if we wanted open caskets.

BETH: He assured me that with modern plastic reconstruction, and some make-up...he promised me, you'd never see the wounds. The caskets were closed.

FRAN: Billy Lazier...a neighboring farmer...

BETH: Three members of the police department...

FRAN: My old teachers from elementary school...Carla Whitaker, my best friend in junior high...now a beautician in Grand Island...

BETH: Tommy Fingers...the town drunk...even he was there....

FRAN: And the reception...later at Uncle Cliff's...

BETH: The visitors came bearing fried chicken, sweet potatoes, Jello, macaroni salads...the tables laden with food...everyone snacking...looking for something to do....

FRAN: Gary shaking hands all day. People he had met only once before, at our wedding day. What does one say at these occasions? What is appropriate behavior?

BETH: To run out the door...head for an open field and scream!

FRAN: So hard to make small talk...

BETH: I had to do something...so I ate...first with one person, and then the next. I ate until I was so full, it hurt to walk, or to sit down, and then I would go into the bathroom and be sick. This went on all day, and everyone remarked on how well I looked. And did I plan to go to graduate school? Or, what were my plans exactly?

(Lights change. They are now seated in CLIFF's *living room.* GARY, LENNY, *and* CLIFF *are with them. They are drinking tea. Silence. A clock chimes.* CLIFF *looks at his watch, and sighs.)*

CLIFF: Nice funeral, I thought.

GARY: Hmm...yes.

FRAN: I'm exhausted.

GARY: You were on your feet all day.

CLIFF: *(Long pause. He winds his watch.)* I been thinkin'... there's a fellow I used to work with...says he knows a detective over in Omaha...name of Sinfeld...they say he's pretty good. So, I been thinkin' if our local police department can't do any better...I just might give this Sinfeld guy a call.

FRAN: A detective?

CLIFF: Oh, don't worry, I'll pay for it. I just don't trust the dumbbells we got for police in this town. They'll botch it up, I tell you. Always do. Can't find their butts with both hands. So, what do you think about calling this guy? *(No one responds.)* Well, I just might give him a call, yessir. *(Pause)* If you girls want, I'll take care of any details about the house. If you want to sell it, I can handle that from here...know a couple of realtors personally. I think the greenhouse should bring a good offer. Now, the house...I don't know... Walter never was much of a handyman...needs fixin' up.... Besides, folks are gonna be just a bit jumpy about livin' there now...but, like I said, if you girls want, I'll take care of it. You just say what you want, and I'll do it.

ACT ONE 31

FRAN: Uncle Cliff, can we discuss this some other time?

CLIFF: Oh, sure. I don't want to push you into somethin' you don't want.

GARY: *(Rises)* I think we should turn in. We've got an early plane in the morning.

FRAN: *(Apologetic)* He does have to get back to work.

GARY: Thanks for everything, Cliff.

CLIFF: No trouble.

FRAN: *(To* BETH*)* Are you going to be all right?

BETH: *(Shrugs)* I guess.

FRAN: If you want, you can come stay with us. Stay as long as you need to. Right, Gary?

GARY: We've got plenty of room, Beth.

BETH: Thanks.

FRAN: Do you know what you're going to do?

*(*BETH *looks at* LENNY. *He stares at his tea cup.* FRAN *touches* BETH, *lightly.)*

FRAN: Okay, we'll talk later. G'night.

*(*FRAN *and* GARY *exit.)*

CLIFF: *(Finishes his tea)* Well...time for me to go to bed. You gonna stay up? *(*BETH *nods.* CLIFF *looks at her with concern.)* I know what it's like, honey. When I lost my Margaret...I thought there was nothin' left for me in the world. Makes you wanna drift for a while, but sooner or later...you shake yourself out of it...you find a reason to go on. You will...in time.

*(*BETH *nods.* CLIFF *pats her arm, and exits.* BETH *and* LENNY *sit still for a moment.)*

LENNY: Beth, I wanna go home.

BETH: Home?

LENNY: Back to New York. I'm sorry...I gotta get away from here. *(BETH nods.)* I'd kind of like it...if maybe you came out there with me. We'll get an apartment together. Will you do that? For me?

(BETH does not answer. She looks at LENNY as if he were a total stranger.)

(Lights change. LENNY exits. BETH sits alone. WALTER appears upstage in a spotlight. He puts a cigarette in his mouth, turns his head to one side, and opens his Zippo lighter with a click. WALTER chuckles to himself.)

BETH: Dad, what happened?

WALTER: You'll never get anything from me. You know that, don't you?

BETH: Tell me. Who did this?

WALTER: I have nothing you'd even want. Look around. See? Absolutely nothing.

BETH: Talk to me...please...

WALTER: So, why do you even bother? You're wasting your time. You got the wrong house. *(His light begins to fade.)*

BETH: Don't leave...wait...*(WALTER laughs as his light fades.)* No...don't go...

(Laughter moves to another part of the stage. Lights up on the dining room table. BARBARA and CAROLYN sit opposite each other, passing a joint. They are very stoned, and laughing easily as BETH moves slowly to them.)

BETH: Hey, keep the noise down. It's almost four in the morning. What are you doing in the kitchen?

CAROLYN: Oh, Barbara, why does it make my face feel so funny?

(BETH stares at them, confused. They laugh, not noticing BETH.)

BARBARA: You're stoned, that's why!

ACT ONE

CAROLYN: Ssssh! We have to be quiet, or we'll wake your sister.

BARBARA: Aw, who cares! We're having fun!

BETH: Wait a minute! You two don't get high! What's happening here?

BARBARA: She thinks I don't know where she hides it. But I do. In an old Papagallo shoe box in her closet.

BETH: Stop it!

(CAROLYN *and* BARBARA *turn slowly, for the first time, looking at* BETH.)

CAROLYN: Come here, Beth!

BETH: No.

CAROLYN: Why not?

BETH: You have a bullet hole in your face.

CAROLYN: Look at my face, Beth.

BETH: No.

CAROLYN: Look at it, Beth. Don't you want to see it? It won't bite you. LOOK AT ME!!!

BETH: Will you stop! Please!

CAROLYN: It's not so bad, is it? It barely hurt. Really, Beth. It was almost painless.

(BETH *looks at* BARBARA, *who is trying to wipe a stain off the front of her blouse.*)

BARBARA: Oh, no...

CAROLYN: Barbara, what have you spilled on that blouse? It's on your collar, and on the shoulder. Barbara, it's soaking through. What is that?

BARBARA: Looks like blood, Mama.

CAROLYN: *(Confused)* You're bleeding. Why?

BARBARA: I don't know. So are you...your face....

(CAROLYN *touches her own cheek, finds blood, looks at it on her hand.*)

CAROLYN: Why, so I am. Isn't that strange? Beth, what's happened?

BETH: I...I...I don't know....

(BARBARA *examines blood on herself, begins to panic.*)

BARBARA: I'm bleeding...I'm really bleeding...I've ruined this blouse...it's all caked and dried...it'll never come out now....

(BARBARA *starts to cry as she wipes at the stain.* BETH *begins to back away from them.* CAROLYN *suddenly throws her head back and lets out a scream of anguish.*)

CAROLYN: WHY IS THIS HAPPENING TO ME??? BETH!!! BETHANY!!!

(*Lights fade on table area. Lights up in another area of the stage.* BETH *is alone in the greenhouse with plants. She is watering several plants.* CLIFF *appears in the doorway. He is carrying a small cardboard box.*)

CLIFF: So, there you are. I been lookin' all over for ya.

BETH: Yeah, I came down to the greenhouse.

CLIFF: What are you doin'?

BETH: These plants need watering, and plant food...you can't let 'em go too long, or they'll die....

(BETH *starts to cry, catches herself, and regains her composure.* CLIFF *gently places a hand on her shoulder.*)

CLIFF: That's okay. I'll take care of 'em. (CLIFF *takes the watering can from her.*) You go on, finish gettin' packed. Don't you worry. I won't let the greenhouse fall into ruin. You go on.

BETH: There's fresh potting soil under those cabinets, and some peat moss in that plastic bin over there....

CLIFF: Honey, don't you worry. I'll figure it out. Margaret and I had our own garden for twenty-three

ACT ONE

years. I got a green thumb. (CLIFF *finishes watering the plants.* BETH *looks at the items in the cardboard box.)* Oh, I put some stuff in that cardboard box you might want. Mostly personal things...you know...some pictures I have...some old letters, that sort of thing. You can have 'em if you want. That there is Walter's Purple Heart Medal from Korea. Thought you might like that.

BETH: Thanks, Uncle Cliff. *(*BETH *finds the Zippo. She looks at the lighter, opening and closing it.* CLIFF *watches her.* BETH *wipes a tear away. She puts the lighter in her pocket.)* Why did it have to happen?

CLIFF: I don't know. But I promise you, I'm gonna find out. I won't rest 'til I get to the bottom of it. You and me, Beth, we ain't quitters. Just a matter of time, that's all.

*(*LENNY *appears, carrying a suitcase.* BETH *looks at* LENNY.*)*

LENNY: Beth? Are you finished packing?

BETH: Yes, I guess so.

LENNY: I wanna go now. Okay? Beth?

*(*BETH *stares into space. Lights fade on the greenhouse area. In darkness, the sound of a brush scrubbing the floor. Lights up on the chalk outlines on the floor.* CAROLYN *is on her knees by the outline of her own body on the floor.* CAROLYN *has a bucket and a scrub brush, and she scrubs a spot on the floor near the outline of her head.* BETH *stands, watching her.)*

BETH: Mama...Mama? What are you doing?

CAROLYN: I gotta get this stain off the floor.

BETH: What are you scrubbing?

CAROLYN: I've always kept a clean house.

BETH: Mama, get up, please.

CAROLYN: *(Scrubbing harder)* Damn, it won't come out!

BETH: That's blood, Mama. Your blood.

CAROLYN: I wish you kids would be more careful in here.

BETH: Mama...stop! It's your blood. You're dead.

CAROLYN: *(Stops scrubbing)* Well, I guess it won't come out. It's a shame.

BETH: Who did this? Who?

WALTER: You father is going to have a fit when he sees this. He'll get his belt after you this time.

(CAROLYN rises and exits with the bucket.)

BETH: Mama...talk to me...don't leave me....

(Lights change. BETH moves to the table area. BETH is now in an apartment in New York. She is examining the contents of a manila envelope mailed by CLIFF. She examines photos and newspaper clippings. LENNY comes into the room. He stands behind her, reading over her shoulder.)

LENNY: What's all this stuff?

BETH: It came in today's mail. A package from Uncle Cliff. He sent me some newspaper clippings about the murders, and some more photographs of my family.

LENNY: Why?

BETH: Because I asked him to.

(LENNY picks up a sheet of paper from the pile on the table.)

LENNY: What's this? A questionnaire?

BETH: He wants me to write down everything I remember. It might be a clue he needs for his files on the case.

(LENNY tosses the form down.)

LENNY: All this playing detective has turned your uncle into an obsessive lunatic.

ACT ONE 37

BETH: No it hasn't. He's concerned...just like I am.

LENNY: Oh, really? Just what do you think he can do that the police haven't already thought of? What makes him so special?

BETH: He won't give up until he knows the truth.

LENNY: Why do you want to do this to yourself?

BETH: I want to remember everything that happened.

LENNY: Why?

BETH: It's important to me. *(Pause)* That whole summer, I was sleepwalking. I was so stoned, all the time, I mean, how do I even know that I didn't kill them?

LENNY: You didn't do it.

BETH: How do I know that? I can't remember anything.

LENNY: Because I remember. I was with you that whole day. Have you forgotten that? Huh?

BETH: I don't know.

LENNY: They gave us both a polygraph test at the police station.

BETH: That doesn't prove anything. Those things aren't accurate...anyone knows that...

LENNY: THIS IS FUCKING CRAZY, Beth!!! You are not responsible for their muders. Will you please take my words for it! I know what I'm talking about. Jesus!

(Long pause. BETH *looks at the papers.* LENNY *tears up the questionnaire.)*

BETH: *(Taking the torn paper)* THEY WERE MY FAMILY!!!

LENNY: AND THEY'RE DEAD!!! You can't change that, can you? *(Pause)* Look, I'm sorry, but this should have stopped a long time ago. I can't go over and over it all the time. I mean, if you gotta talk about it, then see a psychiatrist, 'cause you're gonna drive both of us nuts.

(BETH *gathers the remains of the torn letter from the floor.*)

BETH: I won't bother you about it again.

LENNY: Beth, ten months is long enough. I just can't be sad anymore. Okay? *(Pause)* You know I go outta here in the morning, and I'm at a desk in that printing office all day...I get shit from people I work with, and when I come home after work, I just want some peace and quiet. I sympathize with what you're goin' through, but I think it's time to stop. I mean, look at your own work. *(He takes out a few drawings from her artist portfolio.)* Don't you see it? Look. I come home, I look at the pictures you're working on...and suddenly, I'm depressed....

BETH: They're just landscapes, Lenny. Just pictures...

(LENNY *thrusts a drawing under her nose.*)

LENNY: Are they? Look at this sketch of Fifth Avenue. What do you see? Where are the cars? Where are the people? The awnings? The streetsigns? They got nothing on 'em. Nothing lives here. Did they drop the neutron bomb, or what?

BETH: I'm trying to leave out the extraneous details... so you just see the form. They don't tell a story. They're just shapes...images...massive forms...buildings....

LENNY: Why don't you put in something alive?

BETH: Like what, a tree?

LENNY: Try a human being.

BETH: I don't want to draw figures. It's just the way I feel, Lenny.

LENNY: *(Searching in the portfolio)* Back in school when we had that crummy little apartment across from the

ACT ONE 39

church on Manning Street...with the falling plaster...remember that place?

BETH: Yes.

LENNY: One afternoon, you did a sketch of me. You sat in that old arm chair by the window. You sketched me while I was sleeping. And when I woke up, it was finished, and you showed it to me. It was such a warm picture, full of light, soft afternoon shadows...like those days we spent in bed in that crummy little place...just us...we didn't even care if there was a world outside that room.... *(Pause)* What happened to that sketch? It's not in the portfolio. *(BETH looks away.)* Where is it? *(BETH does not answer. LENNY understands that it has been destroyed.)* I see...well....

BETH: I'm sorry.

LENNY: *(Closes the portfolio)* I don't understand you anymore...I don't understand your fucking pictures either!

(They avoid looking at each other. Lights fade.)

(Chicago lakefront, winter. BETH and FRAN sit on the bench, staring at the frozen lakefront.)

FRAN: It's beautiful.

BETH: What is?

FRAN: The lake. I love it when it's nearly frozen.

BETH: If we don't get inside soon, I'm gonna freeze.

FRAN: *(Recites)* "One must have a mind of winter
To regard the frost and the boughs
Of the pine trees crusted with snow;

And have been cold a long time
To behold the junipers shagged with ice,
The spruces rough in the distant glitter

Of the January sun; and not to think
Of any misery in the sound of the wind,
In the sound of a few leaves,

Which is the sound of the land
Full of the same wind
That is blowing in the same bare place

For the listener, who listens in the snow,
And, nothing himself, beholds
Nothing that is not there and nothing that is."

(Pause) Beautiful poem, huh? It's so perfectly raw...but it's all there.

BETH: What was that?

FRAN: "The Snowman"...Wallace Stevens. My favorite poem.

BETH: What does that one part mean?...The "nothing that..." How does it go?

FRAN: "...nothing that is not there, and nothing that is." You should get that. It's like your pictures...very Zen.

BETH: I don't know much about Zen.

FRAN: I'll loan you some books. It's what you see when you draw...those things you choose to leave out...at least that's how I interpret your work.

BETH: Hmm, that's interesting.

FRAN: *(Looks around)* I sure love the winter...the snow. "The Images of Winter in the Poetry of Wallace Stevens." The title of my thesis. What do you think?

BETH: Sounds impressive.

FRAN: Maybe it's too pretentious.

BETH: *(Shivers)* Can we go somewhere for coffee? I gotta get warm.

FRAN: *(Flaps her arms)* Walk. Move around, you'll keep warm.

ACT ONE 41

BETH: *(Tries to follow suit)* My feet are numb.

FRAN: C'mon...jump up and down...flap your arms...the air is good for you.

BETH: You're nuts. I feel like the Kee-Kee bird... remember? Dad used to say that all the time.... Kee-Kee...Christ, it's cold!

FRAN: *(Sad)* I remember.

BETH: Sorry. I didn't mean to bring you down.

FRAN: Hard to forget about them for long.

BETH: Yes...it's always there...lurking.... So, you like grad school?

FRAN: Yeah, I do like it.

BETH: You always were a better student than me.

FRAN: Gary doesn't like it much.

BETH: No?

FRAN: Oh, no. He doesn't understand why I want to get another degree. He thinks I should be completely happy staying home with Joshua every day. I just have to get out of that house. I tell you, hon...after two years of "goo-goo" and "ca-ca"...my brain was turning into strained carrots. *(Pause)* I probably won't get a chance to use the degree. You gotta have a doctorate to teach nowadays, and I don't think Gary would stick through for that. *(Pause)* I don't know why, but I get restless as hell. I like being a mother, but there's gotta be something more. *(Pause)* And deep down...I think it scares Gary. I might succeed...and then what? *(Pause)* What about you? Where do you go now?

BETH: *(Shrugs)* I've been thinking about California.

FRAN: Oh? What's there?

BETH: It's far away.

FRAN: What would you do out there?

BETH: I applied for a residency in an artists' colony—Garland Mountain. It's in the high desert. You get your own cabin...very isolated...no distractions....

FRAN: And no people.

BETH: I suppose. They haven't accepted me yet. So, we'll see.

FRAN: You aren't going to find what you're looking for on top of some mountain.

BETH: I just feel like I have to keep moving, you know? I feel like if I sit in one spot too long, well, I don't know what will happen.

FRAN: I worry about you.

BETH: I'm okay...really.

(FRAN *watches her.* BETH *is absentmindedly opening and closing the Zippo lighter, lost in thought.*)

FRAN: I wish Uncle Cliff hadn't sent you those things about the murders. We have to put it behind us.

BETH: No, I need to remember.

FRAN: Why?

BETH: I have to know what's real. I was stoned that whole summer. There's these gaps in my memory. I don't know what parts I imagine...what things really did happen....

FRAN: It can eat you up, Beth. *(Pause)* I know it's been harder for you. At least, I had some semblance of normal family life to go home to when it was over. It helped me put distance between myself and that awful time.

BETH: I think about Mom and Dad all the time. And Barbara, too. I wonder if people whose families are alive spend half as much time thinking about them.

(FRAN *looks at* BETH *with concern. Lights fade. Lights up in the table area.* CAROLYN *stands by the dinner table.*)

ACT ONE

CAROLYN: Bethany, will you get down here to this table right this minute! BETHANY! I will count to ten, and you had better be down here, young lady. One, two, three, four, five...six...(BETH *enters.*) Sit down.

BETH: Sorry. I was up in my room. I didn't hear you.

CAROLYN: Sit down. Eat your dinner. (BETH *sits.*) What was so all-fired important up there?

BETH: I was working on a drawing. Where is everyone?

CAROLYN: We've already had our supper. We got tired of waiting for you. Well, go on...eat. (BETH *looks at the food, does not eat.*) Something the matter?

BETH: It's cold.

CAROLYN: Well, I wonder why. *(She starts out, stops, looks at* BETH.*)* And please, sit up straight. You always slouch.

(Reluctantly, BETH *sits up straight.* CAROLYN *exits in disgust.* BETH *looks at her plate. Lights change. The table becomes the table in* FRAN's *house in Evanston, Illinois.* FRAN *sets the table with placemats and a basket of breadsticks.)*

FRAN: Oh, you're exaggerating. It wasn't really like that. Most of the meals I remember were all of us sitting around the table in stony silence.

BETH: Why can't I remember the good things?

FRAN: My life there wasn't all roses either, you know.

BETH: But you got out when you got married. I was stuck there.

FRAN: And you're still angry with them. What good does all that anger do you now?

BETH: I loved them.

FRAN: And hard as it may be to believe sometimes, they loved you too. They were not perfect. They were just people.

(GARY *enters, and sits at the head of the table.*)

GARY: Mmm. Smells good. What are we having?

FRAN: Pot roast and salad.

GARY: Great...(*He senses the mood in the room.*) Am I interrupting something?

FRAN: We're just talking....

GARY: By the darkening gloom in the air, I don't need to ask what about. Same old story, huh?

FRAN: How's Joshua?

GARY: Fine. I changed him, gave his bottle, put him to bed. He's happy. (*They begin to eat their salad in silence.* GARY, *however, is itching to talk.*) If we can get a sitter, there's a new Fellini at the Biograph.

BETH: Not me...I'm tired.

(GARY *glares at* BETH *with annoyance.*)

FRAN: Maybe later in the week. I have to study tonight.

GARY: I see. Well, maybe we can watch some TV later.

FRAN: We'll see.

GARY: (*After a pause*) How's school?

FRAN: Busy.

GARY: Humm, that's interesting. (*To* BETH) And you? Anything to share?

BETH: Not really. I took a nap...went for a walk.

GARY: Yeah, I know. Well, isn't that just dandy. (*Long pause*) Maybe you want to hear about my day, huh? Two guys in my firm got huge bonuses and promotions this week. Harvard MBAs. Typical. They'll get all the prime accounts now. And I went to a sales rep meeting totally unprepared. Everyone in the board room knew it. With any luck I won't get a single new account until spring. *(Long pause)* I guess we won't be buying the sailboat this year. Too bad. *(Growing bitterness)* In fact, we might even start thinking about selling one of the cars. Unless we get some more money coming in, we can start thinking about a second mortgage.

FRAN: Things will get better.

GARY: I'm just saying we've got a lot of bills piling up...Joshua...your tuition...an extra mouth to feed...and seeing how I'm the only one working in this house....

FRAN: Gary, cool it!

BETH: I'll be going to California soon.

GARY: Oh, is that so? When are you leaving?

FRAN: Shut up!

GARY: And what are you going to do for money? You got rich relatives out there you can sponge off?

FRAN: Dammit, Gary!

BETH: *(Rises)* I'll go tomorrow. Is that soon enough for you? *(She leaves the table.)*

FRAN: Beth! Beth...come back. *(Turns to* GARY*)* You apologize to her, now!

GARY: No. I got some rights in my own house. I'm married to you, not her. She's been here long enough. Look at what's happening to us.

FRAN: That is not her fault!

GARY: Will you wake up and look! *(*FRAN *rises, goes after* BETH.*)* Jesus Christ! *(He tosses his fork on the table and sits with his face in his hands. Lights change.)*

(Late at night. BETH *is sleeping on a hide-a-bed in the family room. In the darkness,* GARY *enters, in a bathrobe.*

He stands next to BETH, *watching her sleep.* GARY *notices a shiny object on the coffee table—the Zippo lighter. He picks up the lighter, finds a cigarette in the pocket of his robe. Upstage,* WALTER *appears in light.* WALTER *opens his Zippo with a click.* GARY *opens his Zippo with a click at the same time. Both light cigarettes, and snap lighters shut.* WALTER's *light fades.* BETH *wakes suddenly, sits up.)*

BETH: What...who's there?

(GARY *lights the Zippo so she can see him.)*

GARY: Sorry. I didn't mean to wake you.

BETH: You scared me. Where's Fran?

GARY: Sleeping.

BETH: *(Notices the lighter.)* Where'd you get that?

GARY: Right here. I needed a light.

BETH: That was my father's lighter.

GARY: I know.

BETH: *(Grabs the lighter)* Give it to me! It's mine.

GARY: Relax, I wasn't going to steal it.

(GARY *sits on the end of her bed.)*

BETH: What do you want?

GARY: Nothing. I couldn't sleep. Fran's snoring...so I came down. *(Pause)* Look, tonight at dinner...I didn't mean to take it out on you.

BETH: Okay.

GARY: I've got a lot of pressure at work.

BETH: I've been here two months. It's time for me to go.

GARY: Yeah. *(Offers his cigarette)* You want a drag?

BETH: No, thanks.

GARY: How about a drink?

BETH: No.

ACT ONE 47

GARY: You know, in all the time you've been here, I don't think you got to know me very well. We never had much chance to just sit and talk. I'm really not a bad guy once you get to know me.

BETH: Gary, I'm tired. Why don't you leave me alone, okay?

GARY: Sure...sure. You're always tired, aren't you? *(Gestures out front)* You know that sketch you did last month...that picture you gave us for an anniversary present? That one, over there. See it? *(BETH turns and looks at the picture.)* That drawing of our house. This house. *(Pause)* It's a hard picture to live with. I don't mean it's bad art, no, don't get me wrong. It's good craftsmanship...sure...but it sorta gets on my nerves. I think it's the shadow on the right side of the house. That's what bothers me. See that shadow? When I look at it, I say to myself...what the hell is that shadow? Where is it coming from?

BETH: It's a shadow of a tree...its leaves. The tree is not in the drawing.

GARY: Oh, I know that. That's the logical explanation. I used to think it was a tree shadow...at first...and then, it began to...*(As GARY continues to talk, he moves behind BETH, and stands behind her talking in her ear. BETH is transfixed on the drawing he is describing out front.)* resemble a face...then a whole bunch of faces...and maybe I see the outline of a dog in the foreground, I dunno. It keeps changing every time I look at it. You know how when you look at clouds... they seem to be things that they're not? Well, that shadow is like that...and lately, it's not even a shadow. You know what it is? It's a stain. Yeah...like a blood stain...and it's ugly...and it keeps getting darker...and it gets...fucking oppressive! There's this blood stain creeping down the side of my house, and I don't like it. I don't want to see it. I hate that fucking picture. I wanna tear it out of the frame, and burn it up!

BETH: Then, why don't you?

GARY: I can't...'cause Fran loves it. It's her. You know what I mean? And I love her. See? That's all I got. *(Pause)* How come everything you touch has death on it? *(GARY pulls a revolver from his pocket, and aims the gun directly at the back of BETH's head. Her eyes widen as she realizes what is happening.)* I think now it's your turn!

(GARY cocks the hammer of the gun. BETH puts her hands to her face and screams.)

BETH: NOOO!

(GARY vanishes into the darkness. BETH turns quickly, and finds that he is gone. She slowly faces front, realizing GARY was an apparition in her dream. She stares at the picture he was describing. BETH trembles, and breathes heavily as the light fades to black.)

END OF ACT ONE

ACT TWO

(BETH *is on the floor, curled up in one of the body outlines. The voices of* CAROLYN *and* BARBARA *are heard in darkness.*)

CAROLYN: *(Off)* Beth! Time to go! Better get dressed. We're going to church this morning.

(BETH *stirs.* CAROLYN, BARBARA, *and* WALTER *appear in light in the porch area.*)

BETH: No. Leave the house now. Please. Let's go to the early service.

CAROLYN: It's too late for the early service. You overslept again.

BARBARA: All because of you.

BETH: No, please, you have to leave now. Something terrible is going to happen.

WALTER: You heard your mother.

BETH: Call the police. You have to go. Will you listen to me? Mama! Barbara! They're going to kill you. Why can't you hear me? Run! There's still time.

(*Lights change.* BARBARA *scuffs her heels on the steps of the porch. She stops and looks toward the road.*)

BARBARA: Daddy. Dad. Somebody's coming up the road.

WALTER: Who is it?

BETH: Get out of here! Where's Merridoc? Why isn't he barking?

BARBARA: It's some ol' junky car. It's blue.

WALTER: Who is it, Barbara?

BARBARA: I dunno.

WALTER: Who can that be?

BARBARA: They're coming up to the house.

CAROLYN: That's not Cliff.

WALTER: No.

BARBARA: Who are they?

WALTER: I don't know.

CAROLYN: What do they want?

(The family stands on the porch, frozen in BETH's *memory. The dog begins to bark. Lights fade on the porch area.* BETH *remains on the floor by the outlines.)*

BETH: Why didn't you run? Why? Was it someone you knew? Did he drive up the road in an old blue car? I don't know why, but for some reason, I always think of it as being blue. Did he smile when he got out of the car? Did he walk up to the porch, and ask directions, like a friendly midwestern neighbor? Maybe he said he was hot and thirsty, and could he get a drink of water, please. Did you invite him into the house? *(Pause)* Sometimes I can picture him in my mind. He's tall, thin...long, straggly hair...unwashed. A pair of faded Levis...some old cowboy boots, worn down at the heel, with some silver tape around the toe, holding 'em together. He's got a dirty T-shirt with somethin' written on it I can't make it out. And a blue denim jacket...I can see the butt of a gun stickin' out of his belt in the back. No, wait!...no belt...just a piece of rope around his waist. And when he smiles, and says, "Howdy," he's got crooked teeth, yellowed with tobacco stains. But, he's real friendly...a real charmer.... Can't help thinkin', you've seen him before. He looks like someone you know...maybe you

ACT TWO 51

talked to him once...but you can't remember where. His face just isn't that clear.... Maybe someday, there'll be a moment when it'll all snap into focus....

(Lights change. BETH sits alone on a park bench along Ortega Street in Santa Barbara, California. BETH has her portfolio of drawings at her side. She concentrates on a sketch she is doing. VICKI stands nearby, watching her draw. VICKI wears jeans, a T-shirt with "Go Fly a Kite" on the front, and bracelets of every imaginable style on both her arms. VICKI watches BETH for a moment.)

VICKI: That's my van.

BETH: Huh?

VICKI: My van. The blue Econoline parked across the street, with the kites flying. You put my van in your picture.

BETH: Oh...yes.

VICKI: 'Cept you didn't put the kites in.

BETH: They were the wrong shape for the composition.

VICKI: Oh! You're a pretty good artist, huh?

BETH: I don't know. What do you think?

VICKI: I ain't no critic, but you could probably sell it to someone. But, you'd do a lot better with the tourists if you did sunsets, or seagulls, that kind of stuff. I know a guy who does two-minute charcoal caricatures down at Laguna. The guy makes a fortune, I tell you.

BETH: I don't do portraits.

VICKI: Too bad, 'cause that's where the bread is. Hey, what's your name?

BETH: Beth.

VICKI: Beth...that's a pretty cool name.

(VICKI looks at BETH's drawing. BETH stares at the tattoos on VICKI's arms with morbid fascination. VICKI notices her staring. Embarrassed, BETH looks away.)

BETH: Sorry, I'm just curious about what your tattoos say.

VICKI: Just some old gang shit. Got 'em in jail, handmade. They don't mean nothing no more.

BETH: You were in prison?

VICKI: Long time ago. Nothin' special. I stole some shit, but I'm legit now.

(BETH *points to one tattoo that says* "Vicki".)

BETH: Who's Vicki?

VICKI: That's me! Although that ain't my real name. Are you ready for this?...Vera! That's my real name. Shitty, huh? It was my mother's great aunt or something. Sounds like an old lady's name, right? Vera! Ugh! *(Pause)* I had to change it. Names are fucked up, you know? *(Pause)* Vicki kinda suits me, don't ya think? I used to have this old boyfriend named Vic. We had each other's names tattooed on our arms, see.... *(Shows her arm)* But, then we broke up, so I had a "k-i" added to his name. That's how I got "Vicki." Smart, huh? But, that dumb bastard, Vic, he's probably still runnin' around with "Vera" tattooed on his arm. *(Laughs)* I fixed his ass but good.

BETH: Maybe he had it changed to "Vera Cruz."

VICKI: *(Ponders this)* Vera Cruz...that's in Mexico, right? Yeah, that sounds like somethin' he would do. Vic was a loser. Once I made him a hand-knitted sweater...I even wove some of my own hair into the yarn...put it right there...*(She touches her heart.)* so he'd always know I was close to his heart. Boy, was I a dip! Hey, you got a man?

BETH: No...not now...

VICKI: Broke up, huh?

BETH: Yes.

ACT TWO

VICKI: That's what I thought. Love sucks. That's for sure. It ain't worth it. Chicks have it tough these days. That's a fact.... I seen you around all this week out here drawin' pictures. A real artist. That's pretty cool. So, how come you wanna draw this boring place?

BETH: I like the shapes...the openness...the way the brown hills break up the plane of the horizon. And the light, it's so fantastic in the morning. The quality of sunlight is so different from what it's like back home.

VICKI: Oh, where's that?

BETH: Nebraska.

VICKI: Never been there. Flat and boring, huh? *(BETH nods.)* So...you live around here now?

BETH: The Raleigh.

VICKI: Oh, yeah. What a shit-hole, huh?

BETH: Yeah, I guess so. It's all I can afford right now.

VICKI: The Raleigh! Jees! I spent a drunk weekend there once. Fuckin' noisy...bunch of beaners drinkin' in the lobby all night long, singin' Steely Dan songs. *(Sings in a Mexican accent)* "Hey, Rikki don't lose that number...." "Back, Jack, do it again!" *(Laughs, then looks around)* Gotta watch my mouth around here. Mexicans will cut ya' if you look at 'em cross-eyed. *(Laughs)* I gotta motor mouth, huh? I'll shut up. I'm keepin' ya' from your work.

BETH: No, it's okay. It's nice having someone to talk to. You're the first person who spoke to me all week.

VICKI: First one in English, huh?

BETH: *(Laughs)* Yes. *(Points at* VICKI's *T-shirt)* What's your business? Kites?

VICKI: Yeah, that, and mirrors. You want one of my T-shirts? I got some in the van. I work out of the van. I set up at the beach, or a shopping mall, get a few kites up in the air, and the people gather around. The kites draw the crowd, but it's the mirrors that really bring in the bucks.

BETH: What kind of mirrors?

VICKI: Oh, Coke mirrors mostly. They're embossed with logos around the edges...rock groups, mostly... you know...Grateful Dead, The Doors, Led Zeppelin... Alice Cooper...a big seller last year...the kids love that slob. He bites the heads offa live chickens, ya' know? It's a livin'. You like the kites? (BETH *nods.*) I designed 'em myself. They're just Styrofoam wheels with day-glo pinwheel spinners. Don't cost shit to make 'em. Maybe fifty cents apiece for materials. I sell 'em for five bucks. They fall apart in a week or two, but so what. People know it's crap, and they buy it anyway!

BETH: How'd you get into this?

VICKI: I inherited a vendor's license from a guy I used to live with. I used to be into handmade jewelry... bracelets, earrings...the fuckin' bottom fell out of that market! Copper and silver...whew! Sky high! Lost my shirt. So, I got stuck with seven hundred bracelets. You like jewelry? *(*VICKI *holds up her arm.)* Pick any five or ten you like.

BETH: No, I couldn't afford them.

VICKI: Oh, fuck it! I'll give you a dozen, 'cause I like you. They're turnin' my arms green. Here, take a few offa me.

*(*VICKI *removes several bracelets, gives them to* BETH*.)*

BETH: Thanks. *(Puts the bracelets on.)* Well...what do you think?

VICKI: You look like a native. Very California. *(Pause)* Maybe you wanna make a trade? I got a box with twenty-five pairs of earrings, not the cheap shit, real silver and turquoise...genuine Indian...from Arizona.

ACT TWO 55

BETH: I don't need twenty-five pairs.

VICKI: So, you sell what you don't want.... Okay, I'll throw in two kites, and a mirror...any size...you pick...and you do my picture. Okay?

BETH: Draw you?

VICKI: Sure, why not?

BETH: I don't do portraits.

VICKI: You mean to tell me you draw this good, and you can't do one lousy portrait?

BETH: It's not a question of capability. I just don't draw people anymore. I choose not to do figures, okay?

(VICKI *looks at* BETH's *current sketch.*)

VICKI: So, you're into gas stations.

BETH: Yes...billboards, buildings...landscapes.

VICKI: How come you don't draw people?

BETH: I don't want to. Period.

VICKI: You are very strange. *(Pause)* Tell you what, let me have the picture of the van. This one. I like this one.

BETH: Oh, I don't know....

VICKI: I'll trade...or if you want cash...name a price. You tell me what it's worth.

BETH: It's part of a whole series of...so, I don't know....

VICKI: Okay...okay...I get the idea. Forget I mentioned it.

BETH: I'm sorry. I'm not very good haggling about prices.

VICKI: You don't sell too many pictures, huh?

BETH: No.

VICKI: What are you, some rich tourist? You got a trust fund or somethin'? *(Pause)* You do. I knew it.

BETH: I'm not rich, Vicki.

VICKI: Oh, yeah, so what are you doin' in this part of town, huh? You like the welfare cases, or what?

BETH: I got lost. I just ended up here.

VICKI: Right. And I'm Patty Hearst. *(Pause)* Where'd you say you were from? Nebraska? You run away from home? You in some trouble?

BETH: No! Leave me alone, okay? I don't know why I came here...just let me do my work. Okay?

*(*BETH *turns away, and concentrates on her drawing.* VICKI *watches her for a moment, decides to try a different approach.)*

VICKI: Hey, look. I didn't mean to give ya' the third degree. See, we get a lot of weirdos down here...and like I can see you're legit...a real artist...not some phony, weekend hippie, or somethin'.... Hey, I wanna be your friend. I like you...yeah, I do....

*(*BETH *continues to work.* VICKI *notices* BETH's *purse is open.* VICKI *smoothly removes* BETH's *money from the purse, and pockets it, while talking nonstop.)*

VICKI: Like, when I saw you again this mornin'...I'm standin' over there, pumpin' gas in the van, and I look across the street, and there you are...same spot every day...drawin' pictures. And suddenly I get this very strange vibe like we're gonna be partners...or real good friends or somethin'. Like, I can see us with my van parked down at the beach...me stringin' kites, and you doin' pictures of the surf.... It's a very clear picture in my head.

BETH: Vicki, you barely know me at all.

VICKI: So! I got insights into people's karma.

ACT TWO

(VICKI *spies the Zippo lighter in the purse.* VICKI *pockets the lighter.* BETH *is too engrossed in her work to notice.* VICKI *looks at the portfolio.)*

VICKI: Hey, you got more of your stuff in this thing?

BETH: Yeah.

VICKI: Do you mind if I just take a look at some of this stuff? Hey, my hands are clean. I won't leave any marks on 'em.

BETH: Okay.

VICKI: *(Looking through the portfolio)* Hey, this is pretty good. No shit. Hey, you hungry?

BETH: Sorta.

VICKI: Maybe you wanna go get a burrito or somethin'?

BETH: I have to finish this part before the sun gets any higher.

VICKI: Oh, it changes the shadows and shit, huh?

BETH: Yes.

VICKI: That's cool. Well, maybe I could get us some take out, huh? I'll buy.

BETH: *(Concentrating)* Take out...great...

(VICKI *rises with the entire portfolio under her arm. She walks away. Lights change.* BETH *hears a song in her mind.* "Happy Birthday" *is being sung to* CAROLYN. *Lights up in another part of the stage.* WALTER *and* CAROLYN *are at the table. As the song finishes,* BETH *moves to them with her drawing, rolled up and tied with a ribbon.)*

CAROLYN: What a wonderful birthday. Barbara gave me a beautiful pink sweater.

BETH: I have something, too, Mama. I made it myself. It's just what you wanted.

CAROLYN: *(Taking the drawing)* For me? Oh, thank you, Beth. I'm so excited. Is this what I think it is?

BETH: Yes, Mama, the family portrait. I finally made one for you.

CAROLYN: Oh, Beth. You've made me so very happy.

WALTER: Well, open it, Carolyn. Let's see it.

BETH: Happy birthday, Mama!

(CAROLYN *unrolls the drawing, looks at it with disappointment.*)

BETH: What's the matter, don't you like it?

CAROLYN: I don't understand, Beth. Where are the people? There's no one in this drawing.

BETH: What do you mean?

WALTER: Is this your idea of a joke?

BETH: It's the portrait.

CAROLYN: No it's not! It's a picture of my bedroom. Just an empty room.

BETH: That can't be. I put you in the drawing. I drew Dad, Barbara, and you. I know I did.

CAROLYN: Well, we aren't there. Do you see us? I don't.

BETH: I don't understand.

WALTER: Your mother is very disappointed.

CAROLYN: Beth, this is not what I asked for. What am I supposed to do with a picture of an empty room? I can't hang this up. It's ridiculous.

WALTER: There's not even any furniture in the room.

CAROLYN: Why can't you do the one thing I asked of you?

BETH: Mama...I tried....

WALTER: Another disappointment.

CAROLYN: It's an ugly, pointless drawing, Beth. Like all your drawings...

ACT TWO 59

BETH: No. Where are they? Where are my pictures?

WALTER: They're gone.

BETH: Where? What did you do with them?

WALTER: I told Barbara to take them out of here. I sent her out back, and told her to burn the whole lot. Put 'em in the incinerator where they belong.

BETH: No, you can't do that! Barbara! Bring them back! Barbara!

(Lights change. BETH is back at the bench area, searching frantically for her missing portfolio.)

BETH: Barbara!!!

(VICKI appears, carrying the portfolio.)

VICKI: Howdy, Pilgrim. Did you miss me?

BETH: Goddamn you!

VICKI: Sorry I was gone so long, but like there was this humongous line at Taco Bell.

BETH: Barbara! Give me the pictures!

VICKI: Who's Barbara? Hey, remember me?

BETH: Dammit, Barbara! Give 'em to me.

VICKI: You got sunstroke or somethin'? I'm Vicki. Who the fuck is Barbara?

BETH: GIMME MY PORTFOLIO!

(VICKI gives BETH the portfolio.)

VICKI: Okay! Hey, don't get shook. I brung 'em back.

BETH: And the lighter. Where is it?

VICKI: *(Holding the Zippo)* Nice Zippo.

BETH: Give it to me!

(VICKI tosses her the lighter. BETH opens the portfolio to check the drawings.)

VICKI: They're all there. I didn't hurt them.

BETH: I don't trust you. What happened to my money?

VICKI: What money?

BETH: I had forty-five dollars in my purse.

VICKI: Oh, that money. *(She hands* BETH *a twenty-dollar bill.)* I had some expenses. Gas.

BETH: This is only twenty.

VICKI: I'll make it up to you. Brunch is on me.

BETH: I wouldn't go anywhere with you.

VICKI: Suit yourself. Hey, how come you didn't call the cops? Huh? Most people...they get ripped off... they scream bloody murder.

BETH: *(Embarrassed)* I couldn't remember what color your van was. *(*VICKI *laughs hysterically.)* It's not funny. Stop laughing. Why'd you do this to me? I thought you liked me.

VICKI: I do like you. I like your pictures too. I took 'em to a guy I know, who deals in art. He wouldn't buy any.

BETH: Because he knew they were stolen.

VICKI: He don't care. Naw, he wouldn't buy any 'cause he said they were "too personal, and depict a disturbed sense of reality. They won't sell." His exact words.

BETH: I don't believe you.

VICKI: I'm tellin' you what the man said.

BETH: My work is good. I know it is.

VICKI: It's only one opinion. I like your work, and hey, I'm not disturbed.

(BETH *takes her duffel and portfolio, and crosses to the other side of the road with her thumb out, hitch-hiking.)*

VICKI: Where you goin'?

BETH: Garland Mountain.

ACT TWO

VICKI: Where's that?

BETH: The Mojave Desert.

VICKI: You'll never get there.

BETH: Yes, I will.

VICKI: Not in that direction. The Mojave is the other way. *(Points)* That's South! (BETH *turns, looks skeptical.*) Okay, so, don't believe me. Where's the Pacific Ocean? Over there, right? So, then, which way is South?

(BETH realizes VICKI is right. BETH crosses the road to the correct side. She sticks out her thumb to hitch a ride.)

VICKI: Why go to the desert?

BETH: To get away from you.

VICKI: C'mon, I'll give you a lift as far as L.A. You can get a bus from there.

BETH: I'd rather hitch.

VICKI: You can't hitch to the Mojave. There's coyotes and stuff.

BETH: I'll survive.

VICKI: You don't wanna go to the Mojave. Listen to me...people, like, go crazy in the desert...yeah...they hallucinate right outta their gourds. You can't tell what's real.

BETH: GOOD!

VICKI: Hey, come on, ride in the van with me. No hustle. Just a ride. Gimme a break. Let me do somethin' good for ya'.

BETH: Goodbye, Vera. Nice knowin' ya'.

VICKI: Hey, don't call me that! My name is Vicki.

BETH: *(Walking away)* Vera! Vera! Vera! Adios.

VICKI: That ain't my name! Hey! *(She watches* BETH *disappear down the road.)* A fuckin' shame. I liked you. You're gonna die out there, compadre!

(Lights fade.)

*(*BETH's *cabin at Garland Mountain Colony.* PEG *is showing* BETH *the cabin.* PEG *wears a blue work shirt, faded jeans, and very worn cowboy boots.)*

PEG: This will be your cabin. It's a bit musty, could use some airing out. The bunk is old, but it's sturdy. Table, chair, lamp...refrigerator...hot plate...you got a toilet in there.

BETH: Shower?

PEG: Cold showers up at the lodge. In here you got a basin. It's rustic, get used to it. This is not the Holiday Inn. We serve two meals, breakfast and dinner. Be on time or you don't eat. You're on your own for lunch. Most of the artists don't like to be disturbed in the middle of the day, but if you get hungry, you can bring some sandwich fixin's down to keep in your fridge.

BETH: Fine.

PEG: We tend to get up early at the colony. Use the best light of the day. And we often tend to go to bed when the sun goes down. *(Pause)* If you can't concentrate on your own work, then you can help me tend to the vegetable garden. Hard work feeds inspiration. That's my motto. There are no schedules, 'cept for mealtimes, like I said. You set your own work hours. You're free to explore the mountain, the desert, whatever. And, we got no tennis courts or swimmin' pools. If you get restless, need excitement... it's seven miles down the road you came up. The town of Temeculah. They got nineteen bars and five Mexican restaurants. *(Pause)* I've got only three iron clad rules in this colony. No pets. No TV. No wild

ACT TWO 63

parties. I let people be. Artists come here to work, and I do put a premium on their privacy. Most of them like it that way. Any questions?

BETH: Are there others in residence now?

PEG: I got two writers...married couple...in the cabin up the hill...and a painter in the cabin by the creek... you'll be the fourth. You'll probably run into the others around mealtimes, other than that, they don't tend to socialize much. This is kind of the off-season. Most of them come in the winter months.

BETH: I see. Well, the place is exactly what I need.

PEG: The artwork you sent with your application is up in my office, if you need it back.

BETH: Oh. *(Pause)* Did you like my work?

PEG: I accepted you, didn't I?

(BETH *was expecting more of an answer.* PEG *opens* BETH's *portfolio, and looks at the drawings.)*

PEG: Do you have anything recent in here?

BETH: Yes...some things I did in Santa Barbara.

(PEG *quietly examines the drawings, making little grunts and noises to herself.* BETH *watches, apprehensively.)*

BETH: Uh, that's a series of sketches on Ortega Street. A gas station, a billboard...

PEG: I can see what they are.

BETH: Do you think they're depressing?

PEG: To whom?

BETH: Maybe...disturbed, I mean. *(Apologetic)* I don't do figures much.

PEG: So? *(She smiles at one of the pictures.)* Hmm. So many straight lines.

BETH: Is that good or bad?

PEG: You'll find that the mountain has more irregular, softer lines...if that's what you choose to see...maybe you won't.... *(She turns another page of the portfolio.)*

BETH: Those are some interiors of my parents' house. I did the rooms from memory. I haven't been there in a long time.

PEG: This is where it happened...where they were killed?

BETH: *(Shocked)* Yes... How did you know? Who told you that?

PEG: You told me in your application letter, and you sent along a whole stack of clippings from newspapers. There were several pages of material. I wasn't sure what you expected me to do with all of it. So, I put it in the files. If you want it back, stop by the office.

BETH: Why would I have done that?

PEG: I wondered why at the time. Now that I've seen more of your work, I think you wanted me to see something specific in your pictures.

BETH: What? Tell me.

PEG: I hate to tell artists what I see in their work. It just clutters up their heads with unnecessary ideas.

BETH: No. I have to know. If you don't tell me what you see, then I'll think about it constantly. I'll never be able to concentrate.

PEG: *(After a pause)* All right, I see a paradox. You want to explain the missing part of the image, but you already have. That's evident by what you choose to leave out of the composition. That which is missing suddenly becomes present by the conspicuousness of its absence.

BETH: *(Sotto voce)* "Nothing that is not there, and nothing that is...."

ACT TWO

PEG: Something like that. It's either an inspired accident, or very sophisticated for someone your age to come up with...probably the former.... *(*BETH *moves away and sits down.)* Keep in mind, that's only my opinion, and I could be full of crap. Wouldn't be the first time. *(Looks at* BETH*)* What's the matter? You look peaked.

BETH: I feel a bit dizzy all of a sudden.

PEG: You're not used to the altitude yet. Maybe you need some fresh air. This cabin is very musty. C'mon, let's go outside. Can you stand up?

*(*BETH *rises, wobbly, walks a few steps, finds it hard to breathe.)*

BETH: Maybe I'll go for a walk.

PEG: Are you sure you feel up to it?

BETH: Yes, I'll be all right...I....*(Looks around, disoriented)*

PEG: What?

BETH: I can't remember anything...my name...your name....

PEG: I'm Peg. You're Beth. You're standing on Garland Mountain.

BETH: Everything is like in a dream.

PEG: Maybe you should see a doctor.

BETH: No...I just haven't eaten much...in the last few days...I'll be okay....

*(*BETH *stumbles, and sits on the ground.)*

PEG: You sit right there, and keep out of the sun. I've got some good barley soup up at the lodge.

BETH: Whew! I'll be okay. *(Pause)* Do people lose their minds in the desert?

PEG: People back East thought I'd gone crazy when I came out to live on this mountain. I tell 'em it's all in the mind. *(They laugh.)* You just rest some. I'll get you some soup. You like sourdough bread?

BETH: Yes. Thanks, Peg.

PEG: And I'll get you a hat. You gotta be careful in the sun out here. It plays tricks on you.

(Lights change. Garland Mountain in bright sun. A pile of stones shaped like a small pyramid near the center of the stage. BETH *sits a few feet away with her sketch pad. She wears an L.A. Dodgers baseball cap.* BETH *sits, absentmindedly clicking open and shut the Zippo lighter. She finally notices the pyramid of rocks.* BETH *rises and goes to the pile, and walks around the structure looking at it quizzically. She removes the top stones to see what is inside the pyramid. The unmistakeable sound of a rattlesnake is heard.* BETH *backs away from the rocks. The snake's rattle grows louder, and more fierce.* CAZ *appears. He is dressed in faded denims, with snakeskin boots, a snakeskin belt, an old cowboy hat with a snakeskin hatband, and a pair of leather gloves.* CAZ *has a dangling earring made from the fangs of a rattlesnake.)*

CAZ: Don't move. The snake is attracted by sudden movement. Stand very still.

*(*CAZ *moves to the pile of rocks, and places a large stone over the opening on the top of the pyramid.)*

CAZ: I was savin' him. A big, fat Diamondback. You turn over enough rocks, lady, and sooner or later, you're gonna find one. *(Pause)* Are you lost?

BETH: No. I'm doing some sketching.

CAZ: Are you with that crazy old broad from the other side of the mountain?

BETH: Peg.

CAZ: That's her. You're on the wrong side of the trail. This here is private property.

BETH: I didn't see any sign.

ACT TWO 67

CAZ: This is my mountain. The whole north face, all the way down to those Yucca trees...all mine. I own everything, every rock, every cactus, and sidewinder. And you're trespassin'.

BETH: I'll be going then....

CAZ: Hey! That's okay...you can stay for a while. What's your name?

BETH: Beth.

CAZ: I'm Caz.

BETH: Caz.

CAZ: Some people call me "The Snake Man," 'cause that's what I am. You found one of my holding pens. You like snakes?

BETH: Not really...I mean, I dunno. They're poisonous, aren't they?

CAZ: Yep. This mountain is where they breed. I figure there must be twenty-thousand of them in my land. Keeps most people away. Better than a guard dog. *(Pause)* A man can live off rattlers. The meat is real tender. Tastes just like chicken if you cook 'em right. And the skins are valuable, and the rattle...and the bones. There's nothing that goes to waste on these animals. *(Shows his boots)* Handmade! These would cost you a fortune in L.A. And the venom! Worth more than gold. I milk the snakes, and sell the venom to a medical center in Reno. They turn it into antidote for snake bites. Always in demand. *(Pause)* The rattlesnake is one of God's most perfect creatures. A true survivor...like the sharks...been here since the dinosaurs. Bet you didn't know that!

BETH: No, I didn't.

CAZ: *(Lifting the rock from the top of the pyramid)* You want this one? You can have him for dinner.

BETH: Uh, not today...thanks anyway.

CAZ: He won't bite ya'. I'll pull his fangs with some pliers.

BETH: Have you ever been bitten?

(CAZ *chuckles, and removes one of his leather gloves. He extends a purplish and gnarled hand toward her.*)

CAZ: I got two dead fingers on that hand. I been bit twenty-eight times. I got so much snake venom runnin' through my veins now...I'm immune. Here, I'll show you.

(CAZ *starts to put his hand in the opening in the pyramid.*)

BETH: Oh, God, don't! I believe you. You don't have to show me.

CAZ: But I want to. *(He places his hand in the hole and does not flinch.)* This one ain't even gonna bite. Not hungry. *(Laughs)* Snakes are like gators. You stroke 'em on the back of the head, real smooth...they calm down. A sidewinder will roll over on his back, let you rub his belly...goes right to sleep.

BETH: I wish you'd take your hand out of there. It scares me.

CAZ: *(Removes his hand)* Sure. This one's just a lazy coot. As soon as he knew I wasn't gonna hurt him, he relaxed. Just lays there, lets you pet him...(CAZ *walks up to her.)* You drawin' pictures of my mountain?

BETH: *(Turning her sketch face down)* It's not complete.

CAZ: Let me see. *(*BETH *hesitates.)* Let me see it. Maybe I'll let you stay on my mountain if I like it.

(BETH *gives him the sketch pad.)*

BETH: I don't do portraits, so please don't ask me to do your picture.

CAZ: Why would I want my picture done?

BETH: *(To herself)* Thank God.

ACT TWO

CAZ: *(Handing the sketch pad to her.)* I guess you can stay.

BETH: Thanks.

CAZ: Just don't steal my snakes.

BETH: Don't worry about that.

(CAZ *sits on the ground near* BETH.)

CAZ: Go on, finish your picture. Don't let me bother you. I'll just sit a spell.

(BETH *starts to draw.* CAZ *takes a joint from his pocket, wets it, and lights it with his own Zippo lighter.* BETH *notices his lighter, then looks away.* CAZ *inhales deeply, holds it in, exhales.* BETH *sniffs, and smiles slightly.* CAZ *passes the joint to her.)*

CAZ: You like weed?

(BETH *looks at the joint with mixed feelings.)*

BETH: I haven't been high in a long, long time. I don't know if I should.

CAZ: Go ahead. Indulge yourself. Might make your drawing come out different.

(BETH *takes the joint, and does several tokes, and exhales.)*

BETH: Ooohh! That feels good.

CAZ: I grow it myself. I call it "Temeculah Red."

BETH: Go Big Red!

CAZ: Hmm?

BETH: Something we used to say in high school.

CAZ: Oh. *(Pause)* I didn't do too much school. Eighth grade was about as far as I got.

BETH: *(Passing the joint)* That's probably all anyone needs.

CAZ: Yeah. Well, I figure if you can read and write, that's enough. The rest is just gravy. *(Long pause)* This here is a beautiful view.

BETH: Yes. I like the way the shimmering heat creates a mirage. Makes it look like water way over there.

CAZ: That is water.

BETH: Oh.

CAZ: That's Piute Creek. It's gonna dry up if we don't get any rain soon.

(They finish the joint. BETH *sets her sketchbook aside. They lapse into stoned silence.* BETH *stares at his earring. She touches it lightly.)*

BETH: What is this?

CAZ: Rattler's fangs. (BETH *takes her hand away.)* They won't hurt ya'. You like 'em?

BETH: Sorta. They're scary, but kinda neat, too.

CAZ: I'll make you a pair.

BETH: Would you?

CAZ: Sure, nothin' to it.

*(*CAZ *rises, and walks down to the pyramid. He kicks a few rocks over. The rattlesnake can be heard. From inside his jeans jacket,* CAZ *pulls out a revolver. He holds the gun up for her to see. He cocks the hammer.)*

BETH: NO!...GOD!...NO!...

CAZ: What's the matter with you?

BETH: You've got a gun.

CAZ: Yeah, it's a gun. So? I shoot snakes with it.

BETH: Put it away, please.

CAZ: A gun ain't nothin' to be afraid of. *(*CAZ *walks toward* BETH, *stops in front of her, and hands the gun to her.)* Here! You do it!

BETH: No. I can't!

CAZ: Sure you can...just shoot him in the back of the head.... Take the gun. It's just a piece of steel. Go on... touch it. *(*CAZ *places the gun in her lap.)* Pick it up.

ACT TWO 71

Hold it in your hand. (BETH *lifts it slowly.*) That's right...get the feel of it.

BETH: I can't do this.

CAZ: Sure you can. Hold it comfortably in your hands.

BETH: I don't want to do this.

(CAZ *stands behind* BETH, *guiding her arms.*)

CAZ: Come on, it's fun. Now, raise your arm...sight the target down the barrel...gently squeeze the trigger.

BETH: Don't make me.

CAZ: It's so simple...pull the trigger, Beth. There's nothing to be afraid of.

BETH: No...

CAZ: Pull the trigger...

BETH: No...

CAZ: Aim...back of the head...yes...

BETH: Please...

CAZ: Now! Pull the trigger. SHOOT THE GUN!

(BETH *closes her eyes, shaking with fear and revulsion. In another part of the stage,* BARBARA *appears in light.* BARBARA *scuffs her heels on the porch steps.*)

BARBARA: Somebody's coming up the road to the house.

WALTER: *(Off)* Who is it?

BARBARA: I dunno.

(CAROLYN *and* WALTER *appear on the porch.*)

CAROLYN: What do they want?

WALTER: What kind of car is that?

CAROLYN: Is it Uncle Cliff?

BARBARA: No, it's some ol' junky blue car.

WALTER: Why that looks like....

CAROLYN: Who is that?

BARBARA: It's Beth. She's coming here.

CAROLYN: What is that she's holding in her hand?

BARBARA: It looks like a gun.

WALTER: That's my old pistol. Where'd she find that?

CAROLYN: Beth, what are you doing with Walter's gun? Answer me.

BETH: No, please...

WALTER: I hope that's not loaded, Beth.

BARBARA: Beth!

BETH: No!

WALTER: Beth doesn't know how to shoot. Once I tried to teach her, but she was afraid.

CAROLYN: I tried to teach her to play the piano, but she refused to practice. No patience.

BARBARA: She was always stoned.

BETH: Shut up, all of you!!!

CAZ: Who you talkin' to?

CAROLYN: Sometimes I wondered if she belonged in this family.

BARBARA: Always rebelling. Wouldn't try.

WALTER: She wouldn't do what I asked of her.

CAROLYN: Why can't you wear decent clothes? And stand up straight. You always slouch.

CAZ: Do it now.

WALTER: You're wasting your time.

(WALTER *exits.* BETH *aims at the snake.*)

CAROLYN: There's nothing to be afraid of...it's painless, Beth.

(CAROLYN *exits.*)

ACT TWO 73

BARBARA: It could have been so simple....

(BARBARA *exits.* BETH *closes her eyes. Her arm trembles, holding the gun.*)

CAZ: KILL IT, BETH!!!

(BETH *fires the gun, straight out, missing the snake. She shakes uncontrollably, and staggers backwards.*)

CAZ: Hey, what the hell are you shootin' at? The snake is over there.

(BETH *drops the gun on the ground.*)

CAZ: Hey, what are you doin'?

(BETH *stumbles backwards, dizzy and nauseated. She drops to her knees, crying, and retching upstage. She gasps for air.* CAZ *slowly picks up the gun.*)

CAZ: Girl, this here is an expensive piece. You ain't supposed to throw it in the dirt. (BETH *retches again.*) What's the matter with you? You sick? You smoke too much weed, huh? Shit!

(CAZ *moves to the pyramid of rocks. He aims the gun at the snake, pulls the trigger.* BETH *shrieks at the loud gunshot.*)

BETH: No!!!

(BETH *covers her head.* CAZ *tucks the pistol in his waistband, and stands over her.* BETH *begins to crawl away from him.*)

CAZ: See? Nothin' to it. Hey, why you crawlin' in the dirt? I ain't gonna hurt you. What's the matter with you?

BETH: I...I...could have done it...I could have....

CAZ: Yeah, but you didn't. I did.

BETH: I could have killed them.

CAZ: You couldn't kill shit, girl! (BETH *stares at him, very confused.*) What are you starin' at? You seen a ghost?

BETH: You...and me...we did it...didn't we? (BETH *looks at the gun in his belt, then at his face.*) It was you. You showed me how to do it. You found the gun. You made me do it. But I pulled the trigger. You were just there...with me....

CAZ: What are you talkin' about?

BETH: You and me...in Nebraska...eighteen months ago...we came to the farmhouse...in your old beat-up blue car. We killed my family...all of them...I did it...you and Lenny watched me do it...the three of us....

CAZ: Where was this?

BETH: Kearns, Nebraska.

CAZ: *(Spits)* Nebraska? Shit, I ain't ever been east of Salt Lake. *(Pause)* And I sure as hell never shot nobody. *(Pause)* You're a goddamn looney tune. You know that?

BETH: *(Face in hands)* What is happening to me?

CAZ: And I ain't got no blue car. I got a red pick-up truck.

(*Slowly,* BETH *gets to her feet, and picks up her sketch pad.*)

BETH: I...I have to go...now.

CAZ: Yeah, I think maybe you better go.

(BETH *looks at* CAZ *for a moment.*)

BETH: I'm sorry...I...I thought you were somebody else. I don't even know you.

CAZ: You sure as hell don't! (BETH *stumbles away.*) And you tell that crazy ol' broad to keep you loonies offa my mountain. You tell her! This here is private property!

(*Lights fade. A dying campfire outside* BETH's *cabin, before sunrise.* BETH *sits on the ground by the fire. She drinks a mug of hot tea. Her portfolio is at her side.* BETH *looks through some of her old drawings, brooding. She sets the*

ACT TWO 75

drawings aside, tucks her knees under chin, and stares into the campfire. PEG *comes up to her carrying a blanket.* PEG *drapes the blanket around* BETH's *shoulders.* BETH *is oblivious.)*

PEG: Gettin' chilly. You want some more tea?

BETH: No, thanks.

(PEG *stands for a moment, gazing off toward the desert. She sighs.)*

PEG: Sun will be coming up soon. It turns this whole valley pink and indigo. I love the stillness, just before it gets light. *(Pause)* When I came out here the first time, there wasn't even a town down there. You could sit on this mountainside, and not see more than a handful of electric lights, from one ranch to the next. Hundreds of miles of open desert, stretching out of sight. Then, they built the highways. If the wind is still, you can hear the diesels churning up the road to L.A. The land is changing. Like everything else in this world. *(*PEG *looks at* BETH.*)* What are you thinking about?

BETH: An old farmhouse in Nebraska. *(Looks out at the desert)* I envy the tumbleweeds. They roll back and forth out there. Never have touched down for very long. They have no home.

PEG: When will you be leaving?

BETH: Soon.

PEG: Have you got somewhere to go? Some family?

BETH: *(Sharp)* I haven't got a family. They're all dead!

PEG: *(After a pause)* I thought you had a sister in Chicago.

(BETH *looks at* PEG, *realizes this is true.)*

BETH: I guess she is family, isn't she? And...I got an Uncle Cliff back in Kearns, and a couple of "born again" cousins in Laredo. I never see them, 'cept for weddings and funerals.

PEG: And you've got a nephew.

BETH: Yes, Joshua. I forgot about him. That does make me Aunt Beth. *(Smiles to herself)* He's really a cute kid.

PEG: Sounds like a family to me.

BETH: Are you saying I should go home?

PEG: I try to make it a policy not to tell people what to do. The mountain will still be here when you're ready to come back.

BETH: You're disappointed in me.

PEG: Why do you think that?

BETH: I didn't accomplish much...one drawing...that's all.

PEG: But it was one good drawing.

(BETH *doesn't believe it.*)

BETH: No straight lines, right?

(BETH *opens her portfolio that sits nearby. She looks at several of her drawings in the dim light of the fire.*)

BETH: All this work I did before...it's empty...there's nothing living here...in any of these pictures. *(Angry)* It's garbage...depressing, fucked up, disturbed, trash! They should be destroyed.

(BETH *grabs a handful of drawings, and starts to put them on the fire.* PEG *grabs her arm, stopping her.*)

PEG: No! Don't do that!

BETH: They're my pictures! I can burn 'em if I want!

PEG: *(Taking the portfolio from* BETH*)* You're just angry with yourself.

BETH: Yes, I am!

ACT TWO

PEG: Then, why take it out on your work? This is not a thing to do in anger. Believe me, you'll only regret it later.

BETH: Gimme my pictures.

PEG: No. I won't let you do this.

BETH: I hate those pictures.

PEG: Why? Because your family didn't appreciate them? *(Pause)* It's too late to get their approval, isn't it? It doesn't matter whether you draw empty rooms in a farmhouse, or desert landscapes. If you're going to be an artist in this world, it's time you realize, it's your opinion that counts. Only yours.

BETH: When I look at those drawings, all I see is pain!

PEG: And you can't make the pain disappear by burning these pictures. *(Pause)* You just leave them with me. They'll be safe. I'll keep them for you until you come back for them.

BETH: What if I don't come back?

PEG: Then I'll send them to you. In the meantime, why don't you concentrate on the work you've got in front of you?

BETH: Concentrate! I can't focus on anything! I've got so much shit in my head right now, and if it doesn't stop soon, my brain is gonna explode! Right up into those stars!

PEG: If you go back, what do you expect to find? Just an empty house, Beth, that's all.

BETH: Maybe I'll find an answer.

PEG: And if there isn't an answer? What then?

BETH: I have to know....

PEG: You have to know what?

BETH: I don't know. I just feel so bad all the time....

PEG: *(After a pause)* Beth, you have two choices...you can spend the rest of your life paralyzed, blaming yourself, or you can choose to join the living.

BETH: How dare you! YOU ARE NOT MY MOTHER!!!

PEG: *(Quietly)* No...I'm not.

(Suddenly, BETH realizes how foolish and childish she sounds. She looks away with embarrassment, and stares at the desert for a long moment.)

BETH: I'm sorry, Peg. *(Pause)* I'm gonna miss this place...the desert...it's like looking right inside your own heart.

(They watch the sunrise in silence. Lights fade.)

(Sound of thunder in the darkness. Lights up. BETH stands in the drive of the farmhouse in Kearns. She has her duffel with her. She looks up at the stormy sky above.)

BETH: There's something about the sky just before a thunderstorm on the plains of Nebraska. Giant billowing clouds racing across the horizon, chased by the wind. The yellowish tinge in the air, like tornado weather. The heat lightning, the sudden change in pressure. And everything is dead still. The rolling thunder in the distance...the moment before a calamity. The world grows dark as an eclipse...that signals the beginning and the end of something.

(CLIFF approaches. He smiles as he spots BETH.)

CLIFF: Well, there you are! I heard you were in town. Doris Simmons called me, said she saw you get off the Greyhound bus.

BETH: Uncle Cliff! *(She runs to him and embraces him.)*

CLIFF: Good to see you, honey. You got here just in time. Thunderstorm is comin'. Sure can use it, too. We ain't had a good rain all growin' season. Let me look at you. My, you are skinny. Didn't they feed you out in California?

ACT TWO 79

BETH: I lost some weight. I'm fine.

CLIFF: So, you come out to see the old house, eh?

BETH: Yes. It still looks the same.

CLIFF: Yep. I sold off most of the acreage. Land is too precious to waste around here. But, I don't know about the house. It needs fixin' up. Just been sittin' here. The local folks ain't gonna buy it. A bunch of superstitious old fools if you ask me. But, next fall, we got a new canning factory comin' to town. Be lots of new folks lookin' for a nice place. We slap on a new coat of paint, fix some carpentry here and there, we'll get a good price for it. You'll see.

BETH: Whose car is that parked in the back?

CLIFF: The yellow one? Oh, have I got a surprise for you. You're just gonna bust. Actually, I got two surprises.

BETH: Tell me, what?

CLIFF: First things first. You go on in the house and say hello. The door is unlocked. Go on. See who's in there.

BETH: I'm afraid. Who's in there?

CLIFF: If I tell you, it won't be a surprise.

BETH: Uncle Cliff!

CLIFF: Go on, honey! There's nothin' to be afraid of. You'll see what I mean. It's just an old house, Beth. There ain't no ghosts. Take a look...you'll see....
(He turns to leave.)

BETH: Don't leave me.

CLIFF: Get inside before it starts rainin'. I'll be right back. I got somebody I want you to meet. (CLIFF *runs off.*)

BETH: Uncle Cliff!

(Sounds of thunderclap. BETH *jumps. She turns toward the house. Lights change.* BETH *is standing inside the house. She looks around, frightened.)*

BETH: Hello? Is anyone here? Hello?

(Silence. BETH *takes a few steps. Sound of a brush cleaning a floor.* BETH *looks in the direction of the sound. A figure in dim light is kneeling on the floor, with a pail and brush. The kneeling figure is scrubbing away the chalk outlines.)*

BETH: Who's there?...Someone's in Mama's bedroom.

*(*BETH *stands in the doorway, looking at the figure scrubbing the floor.)*

BETH: Mama?... Mama...is that you?

*(*BETH *turns on the light from a wall switch.* FRAN *rises from the floor, she wipes her forehead with a sleeve. The sisters stare at each other, stunned.)*

BETH: Fran!

FRAN: Beth! IT'S YOU!

BETH: Oh, God, it's you. I thought it was Mama.

FRAN: What are you doing here? I thought you were in California.

BETH: I came back. What are you doing?

FRAN: I'm trying to get these floors in shape. The wood needs to be sanded, I guess....

BETH: Why are you in Kearns?

FRAN: I brought Joshua out for a few weeks to visit Uncle Cliff. He just loves that kid. And, since I didn't have anything better to do, I thought I might as well be useful, try and fix up the house. You should have seen the pile of dust I swept out yesterday. The place is falling down...just been sitting here abandoned....

BETH: Is Gary with you?

FRAN: You must not have gotten my letter.

ACT TWO 81

BETH: No.

(FRAN *sits wearily on the floor, leans back against one of the bedroom walls, sighs.)*

FRAN: We separated. I guess it was inevitable....

BETH: Are you getting a divorce?

FRAN: I don't know. Everything is still up in the air. Gary lost his job. He took it pretty hard, and then everything just went to hell. He finally found another job, but by then I had to stop work on my degree. There was no money to do anything. I don't know what's going to happen. *(Pause)* Neither of us are very optimistic right now. So, if we can sell this place, there will be some income. I suppose I can finish the school in the fall. After that... *(Shrugs.)* So, what about you? How was California?

BETH: A very weird experience. *(Looks around the room)* It's strange to be here. This is the first time I've been in the house since it happened. *(Pause)* I was scared to come inside.

FRAN: So was I...the first time. But then you realize it's just a bunch of empty rooms.

BETH: I was expecting it to be...I don't know...different.

FRAN: Like it was back then?

BETH: I guess I was expecting to see furniture in the rooms.

FRAN: Uncle Cliff put most of it in storage. I suppose we could auction some, unless there's something you want.

BETH: No, nothing.

FRAN: This bedroom does seem different, now. *(Pause)* Like no one ever lived here. *(*BETH *looks at the area that* FRAN *was scrubbing on the floor.)* I got up most of the stain...barely shows now. I still think it needs sanding. Maybe a carpet.

BETH: *(Touches the stain)* It's the only trace.

FRAN: Yes.

BETH: Nights when I could sleep I would often dream about this room. I'd retrace the contours, the shapes of objects, the smells.... *(After a long pause)* I never told anyone this, but the morning it happened...when I left in a big huff...I wished they were dead. Sometimes our secret wishes come true.

FRAN: Sometimes, I used to feel that way too. I know what it's like to love and hate them at the same time, because they're gone.

BETH: I couldn't cry at the funeral.

FRAN: I know.

(They lapse into silence. Sound of rain falling outside. They glance toward the windows.)

BETH: It's raining.

FRAN: Should make all the farmers happy. Been a drought this year. *(Pause)* The rain sounds nice.

BETH: Like home. It never rained the whole time I was out there. I missed it.

(The room is quiet. They sit on the floor, leaning against opposite walls, listening to the rain and the wind. Sound of tiny wind chimes in the breeze.)

FRAN: Listen!

BETH: What is that?

FRAN: Chimes. *(Rises, goes to the window)* It's Mama's wind chimes. They're still hanging from the eaves. I remember when she got them, at the county fair, and she hung them out there. It was the year I went away to college. My God, that was so many years ago.
(The chimes continue. FRAN *listens, in sadness.* BETH *can contain her emotions no longer. She begins to sob.* FRAN

ACT TWO 83

goes to her.) Beth... Oh, Beth... *(Takes her in her arms)* It'll be all right.

BETH: I should have been with them. What right did I have to live? It wasn't fair. I should have been killed, too.

FRAN: *(Holding her)* Don't say that.

BETH: It was my fault. If I hadn't slept so late that Sunday morning, we would have gone to the early service, we wouldn't have been home, it wouldn't have happened. I left, and they were here when they came to kill them. Oh, God... Why? Mama...Barbara...

(FRAN holds her tenderly. After a long pause, FRAN wipes the tears from BETH's eyes.)

FRAN: It was not your fault. There was no way to prevent what happened. You couldn't stop it. *(Pause)* Mama, Daddy, Barbara...they aren't blaming you, Beth. They would have wanted you to survive...they loved you.

(They are silent. Sound of footsteps in another part of the house. CLIFF calls out.)

CLIFF: *(Off)* Beth? Fran? Are you in here?

FRAN: It's Uncle Cliff. *(She calls out.)* We're in the downstairs bedroom, Uncle Cliff.

(CLIFF enters, accompanied by ROGER SINFELD, a man in his thirties. Both are wearing raincoats. CLIFF stops as he sees them huddled together on the floor.)

CLIFF: What are you girls doin'?

FRAN: Nothing. Watching the rain.

CLIFF: Yep. It's really comin' down. This here is the fellow I wanted you girls to meet. This is Roger Sinfeld, that detective I told you about. These are my nieces, Fran and Beth.

SINFELD: Pleased to meet you.

CLIFF: Roger has been workin' with me on the case.

SINFELD: Your uncle has told me a lot about you both.

CLIFF: Yeah, well, I just thought you'd be interested to know that all our efforts have not been wasted. We're on to somethin' big.... See, at first we thought the killers was hippies lookin' for drugs, and then maybe it was somebody your folks knew 'cause there was no sign of a struggle, nothin' was taken....

SINFELD: Your uncle has a pretty good nose for detective work.

CLIFF: Damn right. Somebody had to do somethin'. Can't leave it to the yokels around here, but, like I said, we finally got the big break we been lookin' for.

SINFELD: Not so fast. Maybe it's a lead, maybe it's not....

CLIFF: Hell, it's more than a lead! They got him. I know it.

FRAN: Got who? What are you talking about?

CLIFF: The guy who killed them!

SINFELD: They have a potential suspect in custody in Houston. That's all we know at the moment.

CLIFF: *(Scoffing)* Suspect! The man they got has confessed to eleven murders already. It was on the TV this mornin'.

SINFELD: We intend to check it out, of course.

CLIFF: They arrested this drifter somewhere in Texas, and by some twist of luck it turns out he's confessed to a whole string of unsolved murders, goin' back a dozen years or more. The guy says he killed people all the way from the Dakotas to Arizona.

SINFELD: We made a few phone calls to Texas, and it might be worth a follow-up.

ACT TWO

CLIFF: And, the best part...he admitted that he might have been travellin' through Nebraska the second week of September...the same year your folks were killed. *(Nudges* SINFELD*)* And, tell 'em the kicker...go on!

SINFELD: We've confirmed that he passed a bad check in Omaha on June 3rd.

CLIFF: Six days before he mighta come by here. Now, that's some police work, eh?

SINFELD: Or, it could be just a coincidence. In any case, I'm flying down to Houston tomorrow.

CLIFF: I thought maybe you girls would want to go along.

BETH: No.

FRAN: What we would do there? And what if it's the wrong man, Uncle Cliff?

CLIFF: And what if it's the right one! Don't you want to know, once and for all?

FRAN: Even if this man did turn out to be the murderer, I don't want to see him. I would have nothing to say to him.

CLIFF: Well, I do! *(Frustrated)* Sometimes, I don't understand you. I couldn't rest until I knew the truth.

FRAN: *(After a pause)* It's too late, Uncle Cliff. It's too late. Are you watching Joshua for me?

CLIFF: He's sittin' in my car, right now. He's fine.

FRAN: Will you keep an eye on him, please?

CLIFF: All right...all right...*(Turns to* SINFELD*)* We'd better go. Take Joshua home. I'll fix dinner. C'mon, Roger.

(CLIFF *exits.* SINFELD *lingers in the doorway.)*

SINFELD: Sorry. Your uncle tends to get a little worked up. He thought you'd want to know.

FRAN: Thanks, anyway.

CLIFF: *(Off)* Roger! Are you coming or not?

SINFELD: Nice meeting you.

(SINFELD *exits.* BETH *and* FRAN *sit very still.* FRAN *looks at the windows.)*

FRAN: It stopped raining.

BETH: I feel like I could sleep for a week.

FRAN: Me too. *(Pause)* Poor Uncle Cliff. If this case is ever solved, he won't know what to do with himself. It gave him something to care about.

BETH: Yes. *(Pause)* Will this hurting ever stop?

FRAN: I wish I knew. Maybe part of it...some day.

BETH: Yes.

(BETH *and* FRAN *huddle together as the light fades slowly.)*

(BETH *appears alone in a spotlight.)*

BETH: We went on...and in time entire days could pass and I would scarcely think about what happened in that farmhouse. *(Pause)* That winter, my Uncle Cliff passed away...a heart attack. We buried him next to my parents, and Barbara. I turned his file collection over to the local police. They say they're still working on the case, but I'm not. Perhaps it was meant to be this way. *(Pause)* I try to look forward now...and I see a road lined with telephone poles. A desert road that meets a gentle rise of mountains. I don't know if the road leads toward, or away from, the mountains. *(Pause)* After all...it's not finished yet....

(Lights fade slowly to black.)

END OF PLAY